SECRET
LOS ANGELES

Félicien Cassan and Darrow Carson
Cover photo: Finn Skagn

Félicien Cassan is a French journalist who has been living in Los Angeles since 2013. He has written and edited stories for *Le Monde*, *L'Express*, *CANAL+*, and other well-known publications.

Darrow Carson is a California native who grew up around the world. As an adult, he returned home to work in marketing for Walt Disney Studios, which he left in 2016 to become a tour guide in Los Angeles. His greatest joy is to surprise his guests with the numerous hidden gems the city has to offer.

We have taken great pleasure in drawing up *Secret Los Angeles* and hope that through its guidance you will, like us, continue to discover unusual, hidden or little-known aspects of the city.
Descriptions of certain places are accompanied by thematic sections highlighting historical details or anecdotes as an aid to understanding the city in all its complexity.
Secret Los Angeles also draws attention to the multitude of details found in places that we may pass every day without noticing. These are an invitation to look more closely at the urban landscape and, more generally, a means of seeing our own city with the curiosity and attention that we often display while travelling elsewhere ...

Comments on this guidebook and its contents, as well as information on places we may not have mentioned, are more than welcome and will enrich future editions.

Don't hesitate to contact us:
E-mail: info@jonglezpublishing.com
Jonglez Publishing, 25 rue du Maréchal Foch
78000 Versailles, France

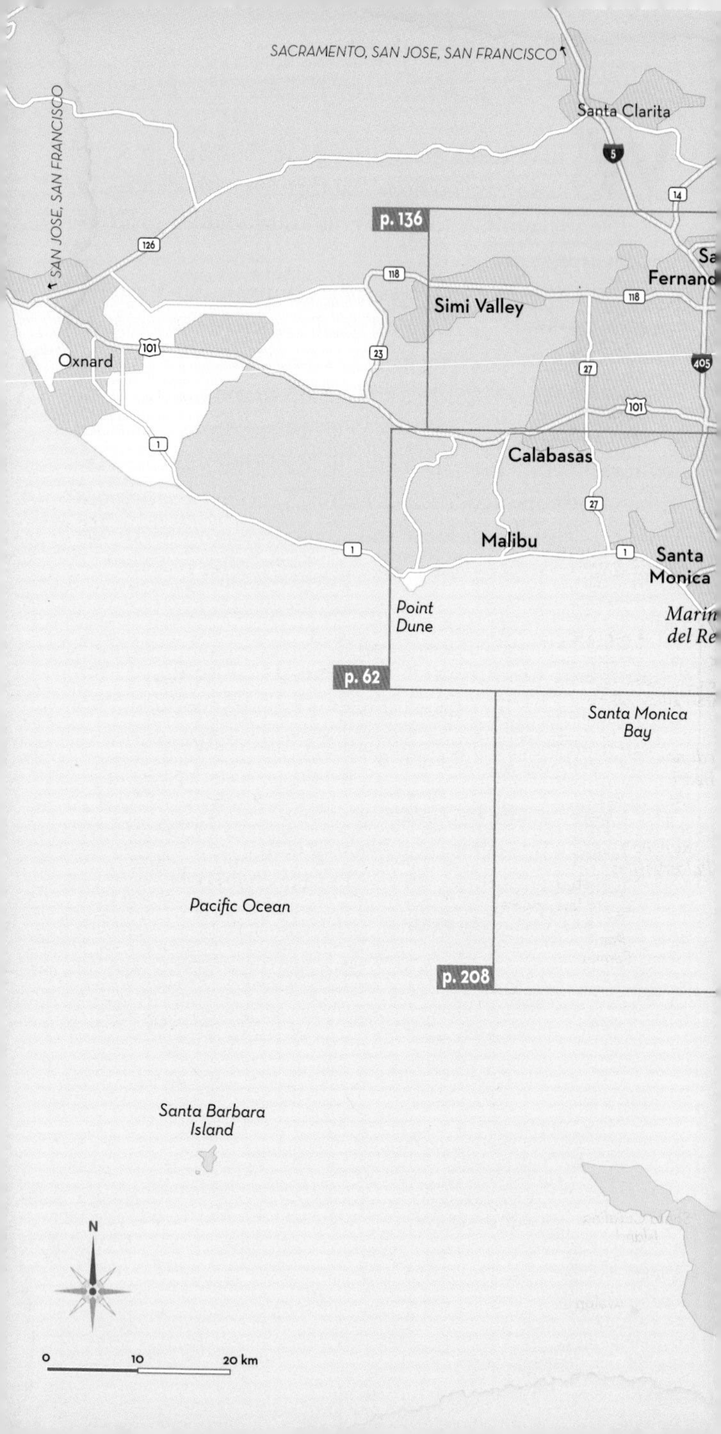

SACRAMENTO, SAN JOSE, SAN FRANCISCO
SAN JOSE, SAN FRANCISCO
Santa Clarita
5
14
p. 136
126
118
Simi Valley
Fernand
118
Oxnard
101
23
27
405
101
Calabasas
1
27
Malibu
1
1
Santa Monica
Point Dune
Marin del Re
p. 62
Santa Monica Bay
Pacific Ocean
p. 208
Santa Barbara Island
N
0
10
20 km

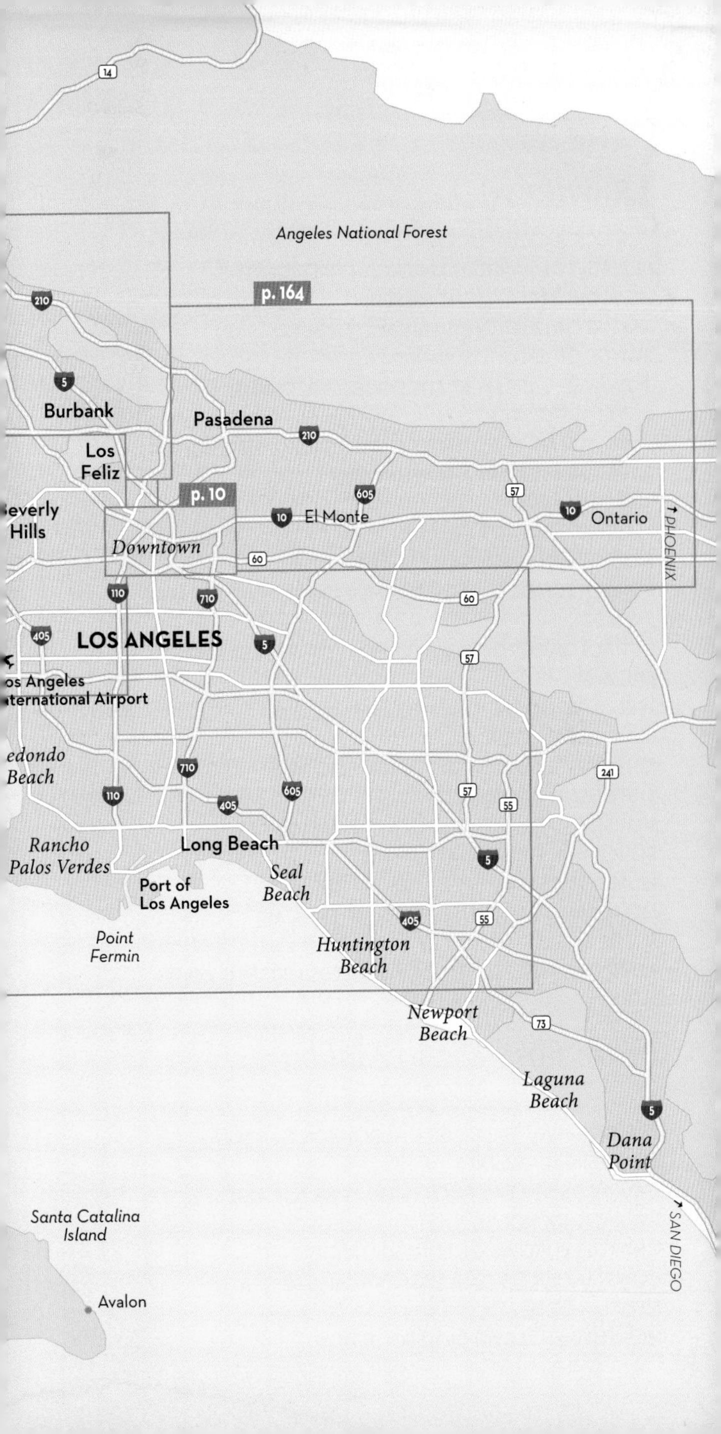

Angeles National Forest
p. 164
Burbank
Pasadena
Los
Feliz
p. 10
everly
Hills
El Monte
Ontario
PHOENIX
Downtown
LOS ANGELES
os Angeles
ternational Airport
edondo
Beach
Rancho
Palos Verdes
Long Beach
Port of
Los Angeles
Seal
Beach
Point
Fermin
Huntington
Beach
Newport
Beach
Laguna
Beach
Dana
Point
SAN DIEGO
Santa Catalina
Island
Avalon

CONTENT

Downtown

THE COCA-COLA "OCEAN LINER" 12
MUSEUM OF AFRICAN AMERICAN FIREFIGHTERS 14
HISTORIC STREETLIGHT MUSEUM 16
STATUE OF LIBERTY COPIES AND TRIBUTES 18
STATUE OF CHIUNE SUGIHARA 20
JAPANESE GARDEN AT THE DOUBLETREE HOTEL 22
AOYAMA FIG TREE 24
OUR LADY OF THE ANGELS CATHEDRAL KINDERGARTEN 26
BARE-CHESTED ABRAHAM LINCOLN STATUE 28
THE TRIFORIUM 30
MAYORS' PORTRAIT GALLERY 32
BIDDY MASON MEMORIAL PARK 36
FORGOTTEN DETAILS OF THE MILLION DOLLAR THEATER FAÇADE 38
INITIALS "BPOE" ON THE PEDIMENT OF ANGELS FLIGHT RAILWAY 40
WELLS FARGO HISTORY MUSEUM 42
BLUE RIBBON GARDEN 44
BELMONT ABANDONED TUNNEL DOG PARK 46
VISTA HERMOSA PARK 48
HOUSE OF MICHAEL JACKSON'S *THRILLER* 50
ECHO PARK'S TIME TRAVEL MART 52
MUSIC BOX STEPS 54
MEMORIAL PLAQUES TO "ROOM 8" THE CAT 56
FACES OF ELYSIAN VALLEY 58
ADVENTURERS' CLUB OF LOS ANGELES MEETING ROOM 60

From Los Feliz to Malibu

GRIFFITH PARK ABANDONED ZOO 64
THE ORIGINAL "BATCAVE" OF BRONSON CANYON 66
SHAKESPEARE BRIDGE 68
"HAPPY FOOT / SAD FOOT" SIGN AT SILVERLAKE 70
HOLLYHOCK HOUSE 72
CHARLES BUKOWSKI'S BUNGALOW 74
CONSTANCE AND CARL BIGSBY'S "MISSILE GRAVE" 76
MUSEUM OF DEATH 78
HIGH TOWER ELEVATOR ASSOCIATION 80

MAGIC CASTLE 82
MUHAMMAD ALI'S STAR 84
HAMBURGER MARY'S BINGO 86
GILMORE GAS STATION AT FARMERS MARKET 88
BERLIN WALL SEGMENTS 90
WARNER MURAL IN WILSHIRE BOULEVARD SYNAGOGUE 92
WILLIAMS ANDREWS CLARK MEMORIAL LIBRARY 94
CARDIFF TOWER 96
CELLULOID MONUMENT 98
"WITCH'S HOUSE" 100
O'NEILL HOUSE 102
FREDERICK R. WEISMAN ART FOUNDATION 104
MONTHLY OPEN DAY AT GREYSTONE MANSION 106
PLAQUE MARKING THE EXACT CENTER OF THE CITY 108
HIKE ON THE LA-96C ANTI-MISSILE DEFENSE SITE 110
SACRED WATER SOURCE OF THE TONGVA 112
CLAY SCULPTURES AT THE BHAGAVAD-GITA MUSEUM 114
MUSEUM OF JURASSIC TECHNOLOGY 116
BIG LEBOWSKI APARTMENT 118
THE MOSAIC TILE HOUSE 120
VENICE BEACH RAINBOW LIFEGUARD STATION 122
THE "OFFICIAL" TERMINUS OF ROUTE 66 124
GRUNION RUN 126
FRANK GEHRY RESIDENCE 128
EAMES HOUSE 130
HIKING AT MURPHY RANCH 132
ABANDONED SETS FROM M*A*S*H 134

San Fernando Valley

BAXTER STREET 138
MUSEUM OF THE HOLY LAND 140
WALK ALONGSIDE THE LOS ANGELES RIVER 142
GRAVES OF CAROLE LOMBARD AND CLARK GABLE 144
NEON MUSEUM 146
RUNWAY OF DISUSED GRAND CENTRAL AIR TERMINAL 148
SOUTH KEYSTONE STREET, BURBANK 150
WALT'S BARN 152
ALFRED HITCHCOCK'S BUNGALOW 5195 154

CONTENT

THE ORIGINAL ROUTE OF THE FIRST CAMPO DE CAHUENGA MISSION *156*
"FREEDOM BOULEVARD" BUILDING BY THIERRY NOIR *158*
DONALD C. TILLMAN WATER RECLAMATION PLANT *160*
DOOR TO ROOM A113 OF CALARTS *162*

Pasadena and East

HERITAGE SQUARE MUSEUM *166*
LUMMIS HOME (EL ALISAL) *168*
SELF-REALIZATION FELLOWSHIP LAKE SHRINE *170*
CHICKEN BOY *172*
MOORE LABORATORY OF ZOOLOGY *174*
LOS ANGELES POLICE MUSEUM *176*
CHURCH OF THE ANGELS BELL *178*
SECRETS OF PASADENA'S GIANT FORK *180*
HIDDEN IN THE HAIR OF JACKIE AND MACK ROBINSON *182*
BUNGALOW HEAVEN NEIGHBORHOOD *184*
ARMENIAN GENOCIDE MEMORIAL TEARS *186*
COLORADO STREET SUICIDE BRIDGE *188*
EAGLE ROCK *190*
FINNISH FOLK ART MUSEUM – PASADENA MUSEUM OF HISTORY *192*
THE GAMBLE HOUSE *194*
"DEVIL'S GATE" DAM *196*
ANCIENT FOREST IN THE DESCANSO GARDENS *198*
MOUNT WILSON OBSERVATORY *200*
BRIDGE TO NOWHERE HIKE *202*
MOUNT BALDY ZEN CENTER *204*
REMAINS OF THE "SOCIALIST COLONY" OF THE LLANO DEL RIO COLLECTIVE *206*

South Los Angeles

VINELAND DRIVE-IN THEATER *210*
HAZEL WRIGHT MEMORIAL ORGAN IN THE "CRYSTAL CATHEDRAL" *212*
RIVO ALTO CIRCULAR CANAL *216*
BISON ON THE LOOSE ON CATALINA ISLAND *218*

ANGELS GATE PARK AND FORT MACARTHUR MILITARY
MUSEUM *220*
SUNKEN CITY OF SAN PEDRO *222*
BAVARIAN VILLAGE OF TORRANCE *224*
ANGELES ABBEY MEMORIAL PARK CEMETERY *226*
BEACH BOYS CHILDHOOD HOME *228*
OLD TOWN MUSIC HALL *230*
THE ABANDONED TOWN OF SURFRIDGE *232*

ALPHABETICAL INDEX *234*

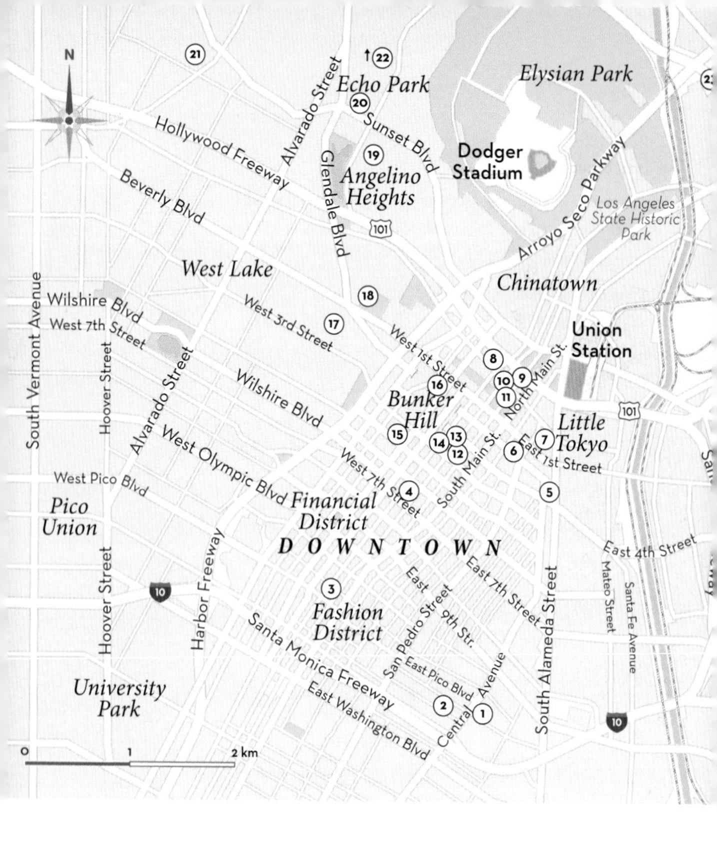

Downtown

1. THE COCA-COLA “OCEAN LINER” 12
2. MUSEUM OF AFRICAN AMERICAN FIREFIGHTERS 14
3. HISTORIC STREETLIGHT MUSEUM 16
4. STATUE OF LIBERTY COPIES AND TRIBUTES 18
5. STATUE OF CHIUNE SUGIHARA 20
6. JAPANESE GARDEN AT THE DOUBLETREE HOTEL 22
7. AOYAMA FIG TREE 24
8. OUR LADY OF THE ANGELS CATHEDRAL KINDERGARTEN 26
9. BARE-CHESTED ABRAHAM LINCOLN STATUE 28
10. THE *TRIFORIUM* 30
11. MAYORS’ PORTRAIT GALLERY 32
12. BIDDY MASON MEMORIAL PARK 36
13. FORGOTTEN DETAILS OF THE MILLION DOLLAR THEATER FAÇADE 38

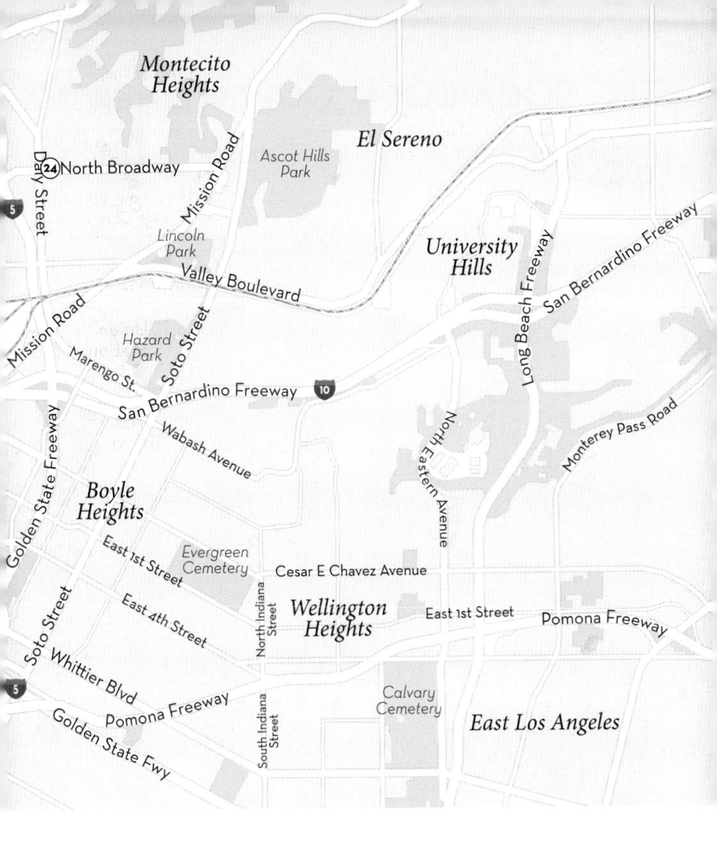

14	INITIALS "BPOE" ON THE PEDIMENT OF ANGELS FLIGHT RAILWAY	40
15	WELLS FARGO HISTORY MUSEUM	42
16	BLUE RIBBON GARDEN	44
17	BELMONT ABANDONED TUNNEL DOG PARK	46
18	VISTA HERMOSA PARK	48
19	HOUSE OF MICHAEL JACKSON'S *THRILLER* CLIP	50
20	ECHO PARK'S TIME TRAVEL MART	52
21	MUSIC BOX STEPS	54
22	MEMORIAL PLAQUES TO "ROOM 8" THE CAT	56
23	FACES OF ELYSIAN VALLEY	58
24	ADVENTURERS' CLUB OF LOS ANGELES MEETING ROOM	60

THE COCA-COLA "OCEAN LINER" ①

Flagship of the Coke brand, well maintained since 1939

Coca-Cola Building
1200–1334 South Central Avenue
Visible from the street

The Coca-Cola Building designed by Robert V. Derrah, a still-functioning bottling plant as secure as a federal prison, is a jewel of nautical Art Deco architecture (known as Streamline Moderne). Located opposite the African American Firefighter Museum (see page 14), the white, red, and black structure has since 1939 been the flagship of the iconic Coke brand from Atlanta, which has several buildings in this otherwise rather desolate district.

Portholes, bridges, hatches, rivets, chimney – all the elements of an authentic ship make up this unexpected gem, only visible from the industrial wasteland street, where tourists and locals very rarely venture.

Note: this astonishing structure shouldn't be confused with the other "Coca-Cola Building" in downtown LA, i.e. the former soulless California headquarters on 4th Street and Traction Avenue (in the Arts District), converted to a shopping center and office block since 2017. Although the neighborhood is now very lively, with trendy bars and restaurants, it's nothing special to look at. The "ocean liner," on the other hand, is certainly worth the trip.

Crossroads of the World

(+1) 323 463 5611

Another concrete flagship, this time topped by a globe and located at 6671 Sunset Boulevard, is a contemporary of the Coca-Cola Building. And for good reason: it sprang from the imagination of the same architect, Robert V. Derrah, who designed it around the same time (1936). The building, then considered to be the first open-air mall in the United States, also resembles a ship, surrounded by a "village" that used to have several shops. The site is now occupied by private offices, but you can still visit during the week. There's even a life-size replica of this very cinematic "crossroads of the world" at the entrance to Walt Disney World, Florida.

MUSEUM OF AFRICAN AMERICAN FIREFIGHTERS

②

Real heroes, long discriminated against

African American Firefighter Museum
1401 South Central Avenue
aaffmuseum.org – +1 (213) 744-1730
Tuesday and Thursday 10am–2pm, Sunday 1pm–4pm
Advisable to call ahead
Free admission for up to 10 visitors
Donation requested from groups of 11 or more

It's an attractive fire station repainted gray, south Downtown, in a desolate and rather unwelcoming neighborhood. On the façade, two images of firefighters keep a lookout in front of a water cannon dating from 1912. The uniqueness of the place isn't obvious until you carefully read the plaque accompanying the aforementioned fresco: the proud firefighters it refers to are black, and this station was segregated from 1924 to 1955!

Since it became a museum, classified as a historic monument, Fire Station #30 has traced the arrival of African American firefighters, covering both their heroic acts and the fight against the discrimination they endured, from physical isolation to the most thankless tasks, including the impossibility of scaling the career ladder.

The museum's collections of uniforms, vehicles, and antiques, while interesting, are less moving than the stories and photos depicting the evils of that era.

A good example: although Station #30 was first located in Westlake North, it was moved "out of sight" in 1924, when the district became concerned about the influence of "black power" over students as plans were drawn up to build Belmont High School. Not until 1956, at the instigation of Arnett Hartsfield Jr (a pioneer who died in 2014), did Stations #14 and #30 revert to the Los Angeles Fire Department (LAFD), despite some opposition.

Although the museum was intended to celebrate the centenary of the first blacks in the firefighter ranks when it opened in 1997, the Los Angeles Times subsequently learned of the existence of Sam Haskins, who, in 1888 had been the city's first African American firefighter. The museum, the only one of its kind in the United States, also pays tribute to black firefighters from all over the country, especially those stationed in New York City on September 11, 2001.

The museum is not much visited and has recently had financial difficulties. All the more important then to pay your respects, preferably calling ahead to be sure someone is there to welcome you on the day you visit.

Another firefighter museum

The Los Angeles Fire Department also has its museum, in the heart of Hollywood (LAFD Museum, 1355 North Cahuenga Boulevard), in former Fire Station #27.
Open only on Saturdays and run by former firefighters, now volunteer guides, it is obviously more complete in terms of collectibles, giving an overview of the distinguished service. But it doesn't have the hidden charm of #30.

HISTORIC STREETLIGHT MUSEUM ③

They gave the city its distinctive color

1149 South Broadway
bsl.lacity.org/museum.html
Museum open to the public one day each month, guided tours 10am–10:30am only
To request a reservation (required), email bslmuseum@lacity.org giving your name, email address, phone number, as well as the date of your choice (opening days available on website)

Novelty alert! Visiting a museum run by the Department of Public Works may not seem very inviting at first, but this mini exhibition hall candidly retraces the history of some of the city's very important immobile characters – its streetlights.

The lights featured here gave LA its warm and distinctive color, oscillating between pale green and golden brown at dusk to its so-recognizable yellow once night has fallen.

This sparkle, created by 200,000 streetlights fixed to poles with wide-ranging styles, has inspired the fantasies of generations of filmmakers and moviegoers.

Think of Nicolas Winding Refn's *Drive*, Michael Mann's *Collateral*, Roman Polanski's *Chinatown*, or David Lynch's *Mulholland Drive* – so many films in which cars and wandering souls ebb and flow, drawn into the carpets of light that they follow, distraught, along the city roads.

Although the bright glow of LED bulbs is gradually replacing the famously cinematic pink-orange halos of these historic lamps, there are still 400 types of streetlights in Los Angeles. They range from the most elaborate Art Deco to highly contemporary versions, from those inspired by late 19th-century gas lamps to the kitsch creations of the 1980s.

Unpretentious and unembellished, this Streetlight Museum offers half-hour guided tours, once a month only, providing a sort of "best of" of these mythical lamps that you'll later notice while exploring the streets. To round off an illuminating experience, don't forget to visit the Neon Museum in Glendale (see page 146).

Joyous little sculptures on the telephone poles

2200 Palms Boulevard, Venice

In your quest for the perfect pole (after the dedicated museum), if you happen to be driving between Culver City and Venice Beach, take Palms Boulevard, slow down and look up. At number 2200, a dozen small, brightly colored, metal sculptures open up the way. Guitar, rooster, bell, robotic skateboarder, friendly insects -- so many joyous figures welcoming visitors to the neighborhood through their peaceful vibes.

STATUE OF LIBERTY COPIES AND TRIBUTES

④

Copies (more or less exact) and a Lady Liberty Building

Lady Liberty Building: 823 Los Angeles Street, Downtown
St. Vincent Court: between Broadway and Hill, on 7th Street, downtown
LACMA: 5905 Wilshire Boulevard, Mid-Wilshire District
El Monte City Hall: 11333 Valley Boulevard, El Monte

Around the world there are copies and imitations of *Liberty Enlightening the World*, better known as the Statue of Liberty, paying tribute to a symbol of US multicultural ideals. They incidentally honor Frédéric-Auguste Bartholdi, the French sculptor behind this monument to hope, the metal framework of which was designed by Gustave Eiffel.

From China to Mexico, from Argentina to Japan, few countries have failed to capture their slice of liberty, though rarely matching the monumental 305 feet of the original edifice offered by France to the United States. Proudly enthroned on New York's Liberty Island since 1886, it welcomes some 25 million visitors a year. The Smithsonian, a research and conservation organization that runs the Washington DC museums, says that Bartholdi's sculpture of Lady Liberty was inspired by an Egyptian peasant he met on his travels.

Los Angeles, not to be left out, also has at least three small statues, including a copy by the artist himself, in addition to the symbolic façade of the Lady Liberty Building. This 1914 construction was embellished in 1987 with a giant tile mosaic by poet Victor di Suvero and artist Judith Harper, at the request of its Iranian-American owners. The mural is called *Liberty Facing West*.

A few blocks away in St. Vincent Court, another replica welcomes visitors in search of some place to eat rather than a safe haven. On 7th Street, between Broadway and Hill, turn right into a dead end. Here, although maybe daunting at night (everything closes after 6pm), during the day you'll find a selection of Mediterranean restaurants with makeshift terraces and trompe l'oeil kitsch, on the grounds of the city's first college, Saint Vincent's. You can't miss the statue, to the left of the entrance.

LACMA (Los Angeles County Museum of Art) has the city's only authentic replica, as Bartholdi's 21-inch eponymous bronze sculpture is displayed there from time to time.

California's only other Statue of Liberty

California's only other copy (30 feet tall, made from fiberglass), is in El Monte City Hall, about 18 miles east of LA, watching over the entrance like a lighthouse.

STATUE OF CHIUNE SUGIHARA ⑤

Little-known Japanese Schindler who saved thousands of Jews

192 South Central Avenue
publicartinpublicplaces.info
Metro: Red or Purple Line, Union Station / Pershing Square stop

As World War II erupted in Europe and thousands of Jews were relentlessly transported to concentration and extermination camps by Hitler's Nazi regime, a Japanese vice-consul based in Kaunas, Lithuania, was issuing transit visas to thousands of local and Polish

citizens condemned to certain death. This was in violation of directives issued by his country in 1940.

Diplomat Chiune "Sempo" Sugihara, born in 1900 in Gifu prefecture, central Japan, had arrived in Northern Europe the year before the war, with the task of monitoring the movements of German and Soviet troops as part of a Japanese–Polish collaboration.

When Jewish families were obviously in danger (despite the regime's lies, encouraging them to stay at home), Chiune Sugihara and his Dutch counterpart, Jan Zwartendijk, started to bypass their respective chains of command. They issued handwritten permits for 6,000 people to travel by train through the Soviet Union (impossible without a visa). They were headed for the Dutch Caribbean colonies of Suriname and Curaçao via Japan, a 10-day journey. Working 18 to 20 hours a day, the two men reproduced exit visas, the quantity each day usually issued in a month, sometimes on plain paper with just a stamp and signature – all highly illegal. Their gesture would snatch thousands from the jaws of death.

In the end, after their Japanese stopover, most of the refugees headed for China, Australia, North and South America, all far enough away from the Nazi threat for the duration of the war. In 1985, Israel honored Sugihara with the status of "Righteous Among the Nations" for his courage and selflessness, as his rebellious spirit predictably cost him his career. He was recognized by his own government only after his death in 1986.

The bronze statue in the heart of Little Tokyo, which celebrates Chiune Sugihara's acts of pure goodness, is as discreet as his life was impressive.

His statue, unveiled in 2002 by one of his sons, shows him seated on a bench holding out a document, while a commemorative stone plaque explains the source of the heroic gesture of this "Japanese Oskar Schindler."

Installed between a Starbucks and a parking lot, the statue faces the Japanese Village Plaza and there's a good chance of missing it if you find yourself, logically enough, at the entrance. Before going into the traditional "village," cross South Central Avenue to salute the memory of this little-known hero of the Holocaust.

JAPANESE GARDEN AT THE DOUBLETREE HOTEL

⑥

Little-known garden on a parking lot roof

Japanese Garden at the Doubletree hotel
Kyoto Garden at DoubleTree by Hilton
120 South Los Angeles Street
+1 (213) 629-1200 – hilton.com/en/doubletree
Open year-round except during private events
Metro: Red or Purple Line, Civic Center / Grand Park Station stop

Los Angeles is home to a significant number of Japanese gardens. They're among numerous green spaces, botanical gardens and other public or private parks that crisscross the city's diverse neighborhoods. From the lush gardens of the Huntington Library (San Marino, near Pasadena) to the discreet Earl Burns Miller Garden (Cal State University at Long Beach), the South Coast Botanic Garden (Palos Verdes Peninsula), and the Descanso Gardens (La Cañada Flintridge), it's all zen. Some locations even embrace the beauty of the Japanese tea ceremony, the architecture of traditional houses or rock gardens, meticulously maintained.

The Western-style Doubletree by Hilton Hotel, at 120 South Los Angeles Street near Little Tokyo, LA's main Japanese district, does not automatically attract attention. There's no indication that the parking lot roof, between tall skyscraper apartment buildings and the hotel's charmless tower, conceals a botanical wonder.

Kyoto Garden, undisturbed by the sprawling city's wail of sirens and urban clamor, is open to casual visitors, though usually reserved for hotel guests or private receptions, including newlyweds in search of a romantic backdrop.

The garden's stream and waterfall contrast beautifully with the aging building.The pool is iconic, an arch awaits lovers, and the view of the downtown skyline is superb.

A real urban oasis, Kyoto Garden is a replica of a 16th-century Tokyo garden created in honor of samurai Kiyomasa Kato. It's the perfect stop before heading to the city's nearby Japanese district, where colorful shops and noisy restaurants welcome tourists.

AOYAMA FIG TREE

⑦

100 years of joy and sorrow for the Japanese community

152 North Central Avenue
Metro: Red or Purple Line, Union Station stop

The century-old Aoyama fig tree, next to a branch of the Museum of Contemporary Art (MOCA) in Little Tokyo, was listed as a historic monument in 2008 (registration No. 920, to be exact). As a shrub planted in 1912, this 65 foot giant held pride of place at the entrance to one of the oldest Buddhist temples in Los Angeles – Koyasan Daishi Mission. The temple, now relocated a block away, was founded in 1909 by the Rev. Shutai Aoyama, a Japanese immigrant priest who labored on farms, on the railroad and in shipyards while he gathered support for the mission.

Thanks to the work of the Little Tokyo Historical Society, whose advice was heeded by the National Register of Historic Places, the Moreton Bay fig (Ficus macrophylla), has recently survived its roots being paved over for a parking lot. But this is far from the only adventure the tree has known. The internment of the Japanese community, decreed by the US government following the 1941 attack on Pearl Harbor, sadly meant that the temple's days were numbered and it was closed within a year. The history of this terrible time is recorded just a few steps from the fig tree at the Japanese American National Museum on the esplanade, as well as at Manzanar, a Californian internment camp and another national historic site, on Highway 395 between the national parks of Sequoia and Death Valley. Healing their wounds as best they could during the 1950s, the city's Japanese people were able to reassert their culture and influence by opening a school in the temple. Since then, the fig tree has presided over a flourishing establishment protected by the development of Little Tokyo. A symbol of the community's hopes and fears, "this tree has endured all sorts of hardships," as Ken Bernstein, head of the Heritage Office, declared to the *Los Angeles Times* at the ceremony that finally gave the Aoyama fig tree a protective screen worthy of its stature.

OUR LADY OF THE ANGELS CATHEDRAL KINDERGARTEN

⑧

Noah's Ark for kids

555 West Temple Street
+1 (213) 680-5200
olacathedral.org
Monday through Friday 6:30am–6pm, Saturday 9am–6pm, Sunday 7am–6pm
Mass schedules available on website
Free
Metro: Red or Purple Line, Union Station stop

Although the angular, asymmetrical aspect of Los Angeles Cathedral (Cathedral of Our Lady of the Angels), inaugurated in 2002, was a hot topic as soon as it began to take shape (see box), the adjoining Olive Garden is an incongruity in itself. This children's play area consists of a succession of animals — mock bronze creatures made from concrete on a steel frame, representing biblical figures with which kids are encouraged to have fun.

A donkey, a monkey, a fish, a beehive, a camel, a lion-- like so many evocations of Noah's Ark and episodes from the Book of Genesis. On the ground, Bible quotations guide visitors through this storybook maze (designed by a children's book artist), set off by the imposing cathedral in the background.

At over 65,000 square feet, the height of an 11-story building, and 68,000 tons, the dimensions of Los Angeles Cathedral are nothing if not impressive. The post-modernist edifice, designed by Spanish architect Rafael Moneo, replaced the Cathedral of Saint Vibiana, which was heavily damaged during the 1994 Northridge earthquake. Now the main place of worship for the city's Roman Catholics, it has a base isolation system of rubber bearings between the foundation and superstructure to absorb quake shocks. In the main entrance, visitors are welcomed by sculptor Robert Graham's monumental statue of Our Lady of the Angels (the original name of the settlement was El Pueblo de Nuestra Señora la Reina de los Ángeles del Río Porciúncula / The Village of Our Lady the Queen of the Angels on the Portiuncula River). Inside, a spectacular, soft milky light streams through the alabaster windows, barely eclipsed by a score of tapestries reminiscent of Italian frescoes. The cathedral, despite criticism during its construction, is now one of the beacons of Downtown LA revival.

BARE-CHESTED ABRAHAM LINCOLN STATUE

⑨

When the 16th US president plays supermodel

"Young Lincoln"
First Street US Courthouse
350 West First Street
cacd.uscourts.gov/locations/first-street-courthouse
(213) 894-1565
Monday–Friday 7am–6pm

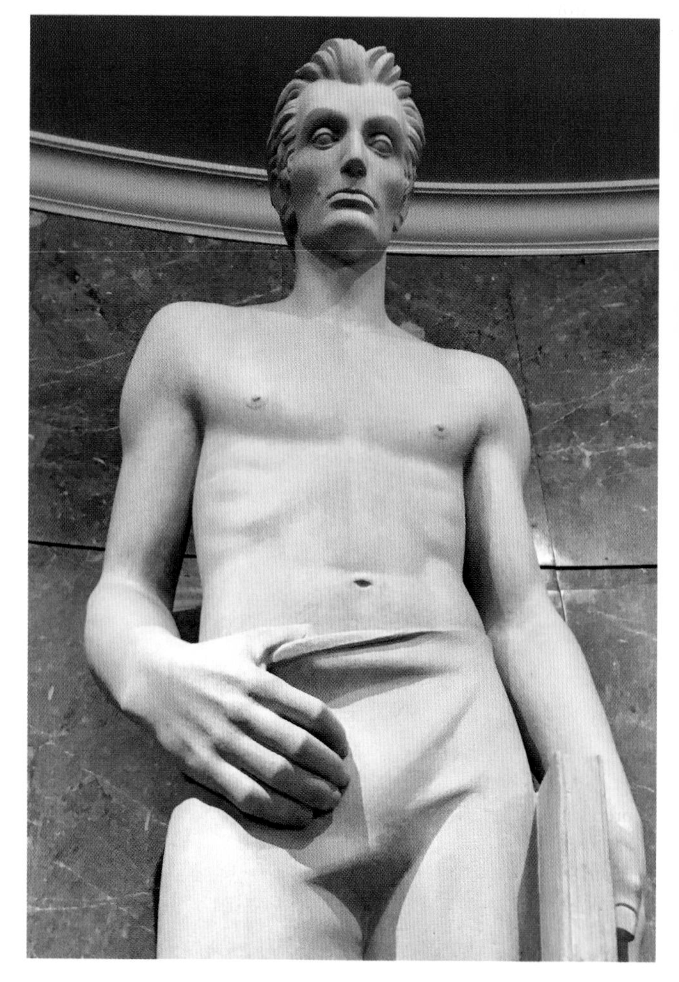

"Modern" statues of great statesmen of the past may be solemn, impressive, or moving, but they are very rarely ... sexy. After all, that's not what they're there for. So it's amazing to see this muscular image of Abraham Lincoln, installed in 1941 at the LA Federal Court, with bulging abs and thumb hooked in his pants waistband like a young and confident supermodel.

James Lee Hansen, art student at California State University, Fresno, was only 23 when he won a 1939 public art contest. But against all odds, the audacity of his "Young Lincoln" was celebrated back then, notably by *Time Magazine*, which described his statue as "the greatest 'success story' of modern sculpture."

"From a sculpturing standpoint, it's better to show the body without any clothes. That's why I left 'em off," said Hansen to justify his creative choice. And even if Lincoln still holds the record of "tallest" US president at 6 feet 4 inches and photos reveal a rather dry-looking man, the artist took inspiration from his own body before adding the "Abe" head. Good thinking there.

Nowadays, thanks to a brief revival of interest that went viral in 2019 and seen through the distorting prism of Californian modern life (surfing, Calvin Klein ads, *Sports Illustrated* magazine), the work has a new tag: "Hot Lincoln." Yet the sight of muscular forearms and open shirt to represent a leader's moral rigor and hard graft is nothing new. No need to go back to Ancient Greece, where such representations were common, because in Washington DC you can see a shirtless George Washington sculpted by Horatio Greenough in 1841. No surprise that it caused a scandal.

Maybe to tone down the virility symbol, Lincoln holds a weighty tome in his other hand. The nation's honor is safe.

Two other "Young Lincolns"

As far as 20th-century artists are concerned, Lincoln's body seems to have been the most inspirational in representing a "strong" president and leader. At Edgewater and New Salem (Illinois) there are two other "Young Lincolns," by Charles Keck (1945) and Avard Fairbanks (1954), respectively, showing him vigorous and hunky, shirt sleeves rolled up, tousled hair blowing in the wind, and blatantly beardless.

THE *TRIFORIUM* ⑩

The remains of an ill-fated, mid 70s public art experiment

Fletcher Bowron Square
Temple and Main

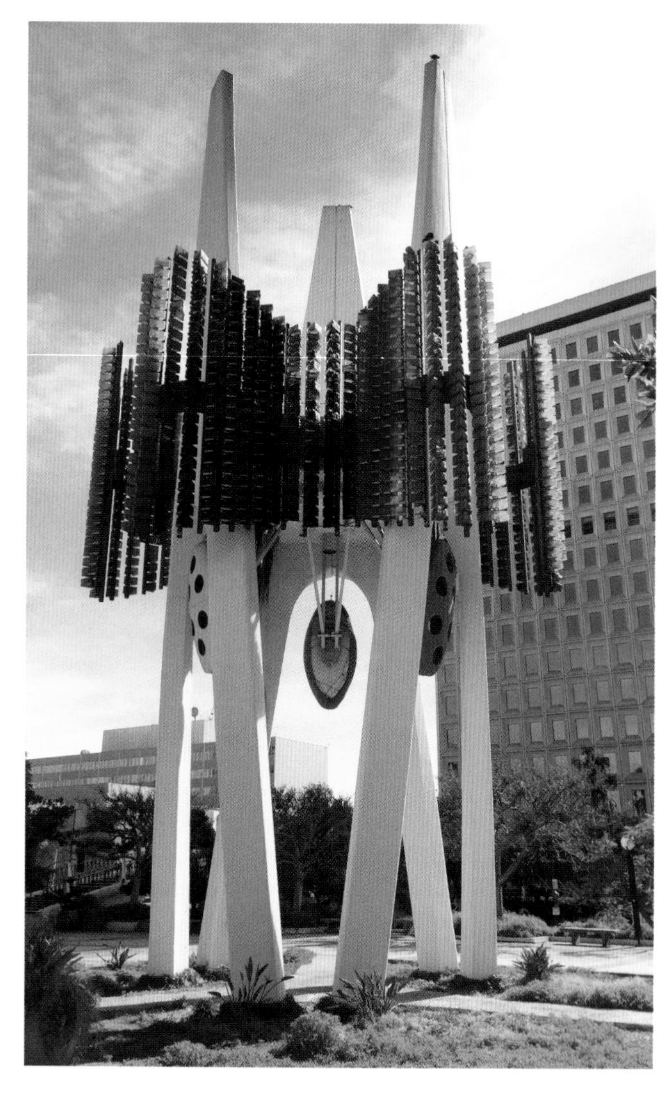

In the shadow of City Hall, atop the eerily deserted aisles of Los Angeles Mall, stands the remains of the *Triforium* – artist Joseph Young's ill-fated, mid 1970s public art experiment.

Six stories tall and weighing 60 tons, Young's visionary "polyphonoptic" sculpture was at the time an unprecedented marriage of technology and public art; an Icarian failure that cost LA taxpayers close to a million dollars in 1975, and has spent decades in various states of disrepair.

Designed to reflect the city's kaleidoscopic spirit, Young's original design called for a massive vintage computer system, complete with motion sensors, to translate the movements of passers-by into psychedelic patterns of light, sound and music. The final product would consist of 1,494 handblown Italian glass prisms, each programmed to light up in synchrony with a massive 79-note glass bell carillon – the largest instrument of its kind in the world – programmed to play "everything from Beethoven to the Bee Gees."

Introduced on 12 December 1975 by then mayor Tom Bradley, a last-minute electrical problem delayed the *Triforium*'s dedication by half an hour – an early ill omen that would set the pace for the sculpture's many difficult decades to come.

Though Young predicted his signature work to be a "Rosetta Stone of art and technology," the court of public opinion seemed to have made up its mind before the *Triforium* was even unveiled. From the very beginning the work was widely disparaged by members of the press and City Council, who showered it with derision: "The Psychedelic Nickelodeon," the "Kitsch-22 of Kinetic Sculpture," and "Three Wishbones in Search of a Turkey."

The carillon is gone, most of the incandescent lights are burnt out, and, in spite of sporadic repairs, what was once LA's crossroads of artistic, civic, and technological ambition is now mostly a pigeon roost.

In the words of Mayor Bradley: "It's ours now, so we're going to have to live with it. More than that, we're going to learn to be proud of it."

MAYORS' PORTRAIT GALLERY

⑪

The great men of the 26th floor

Los Angeles City Hall
200 North Spring Street
(213) 473-3231
lacity.org
Monday–Friday 8am–5pm
Metro: Purple or Red Line, Civic Center / Grand Park Station stop

Los Angeles mayors play hard to get. The City Hall building, logically located downtown, is already imposing enough, but you have to reach the top of its tower if you hope to greet the former city fathers. There are 26 stories to climb, some on foot, and once past the majestic entrance dome, here it is: a formal gallery offering a unique and little-known view of the city, totally hushed yet revealing much about LA history.

What strikes home first, of course, is the changing Californian demographic. White mayors succeed each other like a WASP dynasty, from Alpheus P. Hodges (1850) to Sam Yorti (1961), before Tom Bradley, the first black mayor, grandson of Texan slaves, won the 1973 election.

His stint, still the longest in city history, lasted 20 years and ended just after the 1992 riots. His bronze bust graces the entrance to the new International Terminal of Los Angeles International Airport (LAX), which bears his name. He also paved the way for men of Latin American descent (Antonio Villaraigosa in 2005, and the present incumbent Eric Garcetti). The population of Los Angeles today has a large Spanish-speaking majority (47%).

No woman has yet obtained the keys to the city as, at the time of writing, Eric Garcetti (portrait not yet on display), holds office until 2022. When the Democrat's face appears in the gallery, at the end of his second and last term, perhaps the organizers will adopt an even more original tone.

The largest building in the world with seismic base isolation

The obviously vertiginous observation deck on the 27th floor offers a well-considered panorama of the city's main points of interest. But no worries even at the summit, as Los Angeles City Hall is the world's largest isolated-base building. It's an engineering technical term meaning that lateral flexibility is very important: in other words, the building will barely shake and will absorb seismic shocks even in the event of a major earthquake: all you need to enjoy the view and the mayors' gallery, whatever the circumstances.

CITY OF LOS ANGELES
FOUNDED 1781

COUNTY OF LOS ANGELES
CALIFORNIA

Symbolism of the city's heraldic seal

It's everywhere, yet unnoticed by visitors and residents. The creative enigma is found on government buildings, certain flags and even some goodies you can buy in stores across the city. The Los Angeles heraldic seal, ubiquitous though it may be, is relatively hard to spot and interpret. But it is the most complete page of LA history, because the still current version of 1905 blends the Spanish occupation, the Mexican conquest, and the nascent republic of the mid-19th century.

The castle and lion are from the coat of arms of Castile and Léon, symbolizing Spanish rule over California from 1542 to 1821. The eagle perched on a cactus with a snake in its beak is the emblem of Mexico, which ruled from 1822 to 1846, date of the proclamation of the Republic of California (its symbol is the iconic bear on a red and white flag). The stars and bars are obviously a direct reference to the United States, as California was integrated into the Union on September 9, 1850. The olives, grapes, and oranges represent local crops, while the rosary encircling the seal is a tribute to the missions that Spanish Franciscan priest Junipero Serra, considered the state's spiritual father, founded from 1769 in San Diego until his death in 1784.

An earlier seal, in use from 1854 to 1905, was much more rudimentary: it represented a simple bunch of grapes with the inscription "Corporation of the City of Los Angeles."

The seal of Los Angeles County, the latest version of which dates from 2014, honors Native Americans. An indigenous woman floating on the shore of the Pacific Ocean, mountains in the background, is surrounded by six images, each symbolizing a local specialty or historical detail. On her right are a triangle and caliper (industrial construction and space exploration), a Spanish galleon (commemorating 1542), a tuna (fishing industry); on her left the Hollywood Bowl (cultural life) with two stars above (movie and TV industries), the Mission San Gabriel (historic role in settlements), and finally a championship cow (dairy industry).

BIDDY MASON MEMORIAL PARK ⑫

Slave turned millionaire

333 South Spring Street
Metro: Red or Purple Line, Pershing Square stop

In a neglected corner among the Downtown skyscrapers, between an Italian restaurant and an alley leading to some shops, a collection of unassuming artifacts bears witness to the life and times of an exceptional woman. The monochrome photos of the façade of a house and the decaying shutters of a restored window are incongruous in this modern concrete-and-glass jungle where everyone is rushed. You probably wouldn't even notice the memorial if not for the black concrete wall, inscribed and embedded with pieces of marble, stretching 82 feet along one side of the street.

Between these two spots there once stood the homestead of Bridget "Biddy" Mason, born into slavery in 1818 in the state of Georgia. When her owners, the Smith family, converted to Mormonism, they moved their plantation from Mississippi to San Bernardino, California, as part of an 1851 exodus west that took them through Utah: a trek of around 2,000 miles on foot.

Though slavery had been abolished in California by that time, Robert Smith, feigning ignorance, opposed Biddy's emancipation before setting off yet again to avoid the local law. This time the family moved to the slave state of Texas. But in 1856 Biddy Mason managed to gain her freedom, along with 13 fellow slaves, with the help of a federal judge in a closed court session (at the time, blacks were not allowed to testify against whites).

Once she was freed, "Aunt" Biddy, as she was affectionately known, became a nurse and then a midwife, before founding the first African Methodist Episcopal Church and, most importantly, a school for African Americans. The park and this poignant installation in her memory (*Biddy Mason's Place: A Passage of Time*), designed by US graphic artist Sheila Levrant de Bretteville, are a step back into history, directly to her long-demolished first home. Through short explanatory texts, they tell the incredible story of this unique woman at the very site where her life took an epic turn. After saving for 10 years, the former slave bought this plot and became LA's first black female landowner. In 1884, she sold part of her land, where a commercial building went up. Biddy Mason eventually amassed the sum of $300,000 (equivalent to around $6 million today) and donated her fortune to various charities, tirelessly serving both black and white communities to the end of her life. She died January 15, 1891, and is buried at Evergreen Cemetery in the Boyle Heights district of LA, 3 miles to the east.

FORGOTTEN DETAILS OF THE MILLION DOLLAR THEATER FAÇADE

(13)

The meeting of water and artisans of the big screen

307 South Broadway
(213) 617-3600
Metro: Red Line, Pershing Square stop

In Hollywood's heyday there were over 300 theaters in downtown LA – 22 of them on South Broadway alone. The Million Dollar Theater (which owes its name to the sum of money that entrepreneur and showman Sid Grauman invested in its construction) stands at number 307. Apart from the display cases announcing films and plays, there usually is nothing to distinguish the frontage of a building housing a cinema or theater from the next-door neighbors (often very basic office buildings). Here, on the contrary, the entire frontage bears witness to a mythological story as much as to a very real passion, which seems to revolve around two elements: water and the seventh art (making motion pictures).

Why do these sculptures perched on the cornices seem to be pouring liquid from the roof? What do these waterfalls that seem to spring from the vault above the entrance mean? Who are these "people" dancing and agitating on the second floor?

When it opened in 1918, the building was originally the headquarters of Water Works and Supply, the public service responsible for the treatment and distribution of water in Los Angeles. The sculptures pay tribute to William Mulholland, the civil engineer who was responsible for building the infrastructure to provide a water supply, and who is commonly recognized as the savior of a city which would have died of thirst without his intervention. Water is symbolically allowed to flow along the façade, with the blessing of Tethys the sea goddess, whose emblem overlooks the former office of the said Mulholland.

But the Million Dollar Theater — not content to shroud itself in mythology — also celebrates the cinema in a more down-to-earth way. Sid Grauman wanted, above all, that actors should be revered and that the public should literally raise their eyes to the heavens to see them at a time when the profession was still very much looked down on. A close look at the second floor reveals statues representing the various professions of the film industry: dancer, musician, technician, screenwriter, actor, artist.

The first red carpet in history

Grauman was also the first to roll out a red carpet at premieres – an honor historically reserved for royalty. Ironically, soon after its opening, the Million Dollar Theater stopped showing movies and concentrated on hosting musicians.

INITIALS "BPOE" ON THE PEDIMENT OF ANGELS FLIGHT RAILWAY

⑭

The territory of mysterious elks

350 South Grand Avenue
+1 (213) 626-1901
angelsflight.org
Metro: Red Line, Pershing Square stop

The world's smallest railway has been a phenomenal success since it reopened in August 2017 after several failures due to a series of incidents that the box-office hit musical La La Land helped obliterate in 2016. But there's a mystery that the vast majority of passengers on the orange funicular, a landmark on Bunker Hill since 1901, don't even notice.

On the famous Beaux-Arts façade of the entrance archway overlooking Hill Street, opposite Grand Central Market, four letters in a matching color merge into the pediment – just look up before boarding.

At a time when residents of this wealthy neighborhood rode the two funicular carriages (known as Sinai and Olivet) more regularly than the tourists to literally go downtown (to the lower city), James Ward Eddy, builder and private operator of the railway, had these mysterious initials engraved. They were there to commemorate a rather special group that gathered in 1909 at the top of the hill to hold a conference: the Benevolent and Protective Order of Elks (BPOE), a US fraternity with its Californian headquarters at the Bunker Hill terminus, Lodge Number 99.

Calling themselves – not without a touch of irony – the Best People On Earth, the group members included in their time US General Douglas MacArthur and presidents Truman, Eisenhower, and Kennedy. What began in 1868 as the "Jolly Corks," a private club for New York entertainers to sidestep the lack of public taverns opening on Sundays, grew into a society with over a million members around the world, headquartered in Chicago.

The lodge, at first devoted to aid for veterans of the American Civil War, has diversified in its philanthropic activities (as have the Rotary Club, Kiwanis and Lions clubs), running up against topical social controversies along the way. Women and people of color are now accepted, but conditions for potential membership include US citizenship and belief in God. Non-affiliation to the Communist Party is no longer a criterion, though.

In any case, you don't need to be a member of the California Lodge to board Angels Flight, which has morphed into a tourist attraction run by the Angels Flight Railway Foundation.

WELLS FARGO HISTORY MUSEUM ⑮

Conquest of the West and the Gold Rush

333 South Grand Avenue
+1 (213) 253-7166
wellsfargohistory.com/museums/los-angeles
Monday through Friday, 9am–5pm
Free guided tours, for bookings of up to 10 people
Free admission
Metro: Red or Purple Line, Pershing Square stop

In the year 1852, Henry Wells and William Fargo, the two founders of American Express, set up Wells Fargo & Company. Twists of fate over the years turned the mail, transportation, and delivery service into the third-largest US finance group (and the fifth-largest company in the world).

Headquartered in San Francisco, today's Wells Fargo super-bank, with offices around the United States, also runs 12 museums including Denver, Phoenix, Portland and Sacramento. And their appeal is that they're not content to merely sing the glories of capitalism but to retrace the wild epic of the transformation that went with the conquest of the West. The Gold Rush turned these convoys of men, women, and mail into cashlines, before the coming of the railroad ultimately transformed how Americans interacted with these infinitely vast spaces.

In the Los Angeles museum, there's a replica of a stagecoach in the company's trademark colors (red and gold), archival photos, authentic gold nuggets, a telegraph, tools used in mining, and especially maps, including one of the Pony Express. This was a fast-track horse-and-rider relay mail service that ran from St Joseph (Missouri) to Sacramento (California) on a route once used by Wells Fargo stagecoaches. The local maps of Los Angeles alone are worth seeing, meticulously documenting the evolution of the city.

The exhibits also trace the fate of those men and women who built the company's reputation. Whether stagecoach drivers, bankers, or shotgun messengers (security guards), they were regularly attacked on the road before the company evolved into a bank.

These stagecoaches, witnesses to a bygone era, now turn up at fairs and special events. Financial transactions take just a microsecond to cross the globe (and a few human hours by air), whereas these contraptions originally took 24 days overland from the East to the western United States. It's a starkly impressive change of scale.

BLUE RIBBON GARDEN

⑯

A Rose for Lilly (Disney)

Walt Disney Concert Hall
111 South Grand Avenue
+1 (323) 850-2000
laphil.com
Metro: Red or Purple Line, Civic Center / Grand Park Station stop

The Walt Disney Concert Hall, designed by architect Frank Gehry and opened in 2003, has become a symbol of the city. But high up around the back of the building is a little-known public space, the Blue Ribbon Garden, perfect for a quiet lunch break.

Exotic plants dot the alleys of this idyllic park with its few tables scattered about. An original fountain, also by Frank Gehry, is particularly eye-catching. *A Rose for Lilly*, in Delft porcelain, is like a mosaic made up of thousands of tile shards.

The fountain is dedicated to the passion that hall donor Lilly Disney (Walt's widow) had for roses and for this noble ware. Further along, past a mini-theater that hosts occasional children's shows, a steel-lined passageway leads back to Grand Avenue.

Patina, the on-site restaurant, even cultivates little plots of aromatic plants and edible flowers in the heart of the garden. Violets, rosemary, fennel, according to the season: harmony from plot to plate.

BELMONT ABANDONED TUNNEL DOG PARK

⑰

Transiting, trafficking, music-making ... the beating heart of a bygone age

Belmont Tunnel, Hollywood Subway
1304 West 2nd Street
Always accessible

Many years before the modern metro was built in the 1990s, the Belmont Tunnel, used by 20 million streetcar passengers a year, was indisputably the most frequented "crossroads" in America. From 1910 to 1950 it connected the various lines of the Pacific Electric Railway Company, running from Downtown LA (at the corner of 6th Street and Main Street) to Westlake in the west.

This transit system linked San Fernando Valley, Glendale, Santa Monica, and Hollywood, foreshadowing what would much later become the route of Los Angeles County Metro Rail. Between the two eras, from 1950 to 1990, heyday of the private car, the abandoned tunnel was a draw to the LA underworld.

Now closed up and repainted, its discreet entrance, located on 2nd Street and listed as a historic monument, has been rehabilitated into a dog park: an ordinary lamp pole, synthetic grass and a few colors reminiscent of an old streetcar, that's all.

But this place lies behind many of the myths that forged the aura of a cool and mysterious Californian culture, admired around the world.

Movies such as *The Running Man*, *Predator*, *Reservoir Dogs*, as well as a number of clips by iconic local bands, have featured the tunnel entrance (and the tunnel itself, now closed to the public). Black Rebel Motorcycle Club, Warren G, Carlos Santana (for *Maria Maria*) – these are just a few of the musicians who've frequented this apparently charmless place, difficult to track down but with a magnetic pull.

The most evocative take on this old network was by rockers Red Hot Chili Peppers, who in 1991 made the video for their hit single *Under the Bridge*, a real ode to Los Angeles. It shows Anthony Kiedis, band frontman and vocalist, walking through the tunnel, the menacing mouth of which opens up from time to time while guitarist John Frusciante hovers around.

This globally successful single (the band's greatest hit to date), from their fifth album *Blood Sugar Sex Magik*, chronicles the charismatic songwriter's descent into hell and drug addiction following his girlfriend's death. The story goes that he spent his time wandering the city, stocked up on dope near the Belmont Tunnel, and above all that the spirit of LA was watching over him, which brought him to write these lyrics (meeting with critical acclaim thanks to producer Rick Rubin) and leave his murky past behind. "I don't ever wanna feel like I did that day," goes the haunting chorus. A unique theme for a special place.

There's even a skateboarding facility here, along with a 3D simulation of Tony Hawk of video game fame.

VISTA HERMOSA PARK

(18)

A miniature forest in the heart of the city

100 North Toluca Street
+1 (213) 250-3578
laparks.org/park/vista-hermosa
Daily 7am–7:30pm (dawn to dusk)

The most stunning view of downtown, as well as being the most romantic, is the result of a project to rehabilitate a predominantly Latino district from its endemic poverty, to the northwest of highways 110 and 101 demarcating the entrance to the city center.

A green haven perfect for a picnic despite its proximity to the built-up area, livened up with a few hiking trails and a little amphitheater, in 2008 Vista Hermosa was the first park to be built near the city center in over a century.

The Santa Monica Mountains Conservancy and the Mountains Recreation and Conservation Authority have joined forces with the city and the Los Angeles Unified School District (LAUSD) to provide residents with a place where streams, rocks, waterfalls, and meadows succeed native trees, complete with art installations on environmental themes. The park, which has its own water supply, has in fact been designed along eco-responsible lines.

The 9-acre site, which has become a popular spot for joggers, also hosts a FIFA-standard soccer ground, just down below, shared by Sunday players and students from Belmont High School. The facility was planned at the same time as the park.

But the main target audience is the disadvantaged local community: Vista Hermosa which, thanks to its variety of plantations, forms a "gateway" to the Santa Monica mountain range. Outings with free shuttles to mountains or beach are regularly organized for local families.

In a city poor in parks, where most green spaces are concentrated in Griffith Park or in mountains difficult to reach without a car, this project developed over a disused oil field and a fault line is strikingly successful. Just take a few steps through what appears to be a forest, then imagine yourself a thousand miles from a megalopolis of 4 million.

HOUSE OF MICHAEL JACKSON'S *THRILLER* ⑲

Escape from the zombie dancers

Sanders House
1345 Carroll Avenue
View from the street

This is surely the most iconic music video of all time, a horrifying 13-minute short that revolutionized the art, not to mention its brilliant soundtrack.

Thriller, the song written by Rod Temperton and performed by Michael Jackson, the third single from the album that smashed all sales records on its release in 1982, was already a clever and glowing tribute to the horror film.

John Landis, director of *An American Werewolf in London* (1981), a feature film that the singer revered, would clearly have a hand in the visuals of this story of a girl (played by Ola Ray) betrayed twice by a boy she thinks has no backstory. The first time, with his date at the "movie in the movie," when he turns into a big-cat-like werewolf (the scenes were shot in Griffith Park and two of the city's cinemas); then again in "real life," where he launches into the most copied choreography of all time in the guise of a decaying zombie. The celebrated dance routine by Michael Jackson and his new friends from beyond the grave, filmed in the Boyle Heights district, has become as classic as the track itself.

At the end of this slow march of horror, Jackson's sweetheart hides away in a menacing-looking abandoned Victorian house until he rescues her from the nightmare. Although the interiors were shot in the studio, you can still see the house used for outdoor scenes, almost in its former glory.

Built in 1887 by one Michael Sanders – hence the name – the house is still standing, proud though rather neglected, in the Angelino Heights neighborhood north of downtown. The street is otherwise well-endowed with Queen Anne and other Eastlake-style mansions, typical of the late Victorian period.

Although this is a private property not open to visitors, nothing prevents you stopping by the house for a final thrill, especially around Halloween, when its icy austerity contrasts with the neighbors' opulent decorations.

ECHO PARK'S TIME TRAVEL MART

⑳

A crazy project and shop taking you Back to the Future

1714 West Sunset Boulevard
(+1) 213-413-3388
timetravelmart.com
826la.org
Daily 12 noon–6pm

Specs to see what the future holds, "Pastport," dinosaur eggs, robotic arms, mad scientist outfits, mammoth meat, time-travel sickness treatments, mummy attack survival kits, vials of dead tongues: you'll have surmised that this shop, which takes you *Back to the Future* as much as the colorful lab of a psycho scientist, is unique. But not only because of being dedicated to the sale of quirky objects.

This little "mart" is one of the crazy projects of the 826LA collective, LA branch of Project 826 set up by American writer Dave Egger, author of the memoir, *A Heartbreaking Work of Staggering Genius*. It offers literary educational programs to underprivileged students aged 6 to 18 across the city, with a view to helping teachers inspire the kids' writing.

The non-profit organization 826 National was launched in 2002 in the Valencia district of San Francisco by Egger and educator-turned-author Nínive Clements Calegari.

Its success since then has prompted its founders to open satellites in LA, New York, Chicago, Ann Arbor (near Detroit, Michigan), Washington DC, Boston, and New Orleans. As the launch site was in a commercial zone, local law required "826" to not just offer free tutoring, but sell something there.

So came the idea of including a shop full of oddball items, each more absurd than the other – all with a crazy theme – to raise funds for the programs.

For example, in the Echo Park and Mar Vista districts (12515 Venice Boulevard, same hours) there are two shops specializing in time travel, while those in San Francisco are given over to pirates, the shop in Brooklyn to superheroes, Chicago secret agents, Ann Arbor robots, Boston to Bigfoot (the American-Canadian equivalent of the legendary Himalayan Yeti), Washington to magic, and New Orleans to ghosts. The arrangement is similar everywhere: on display are hilarious objects and souvenirs to rummage through, with playful presentation and wide choice.

Then, in the back shop, is the educational hub of a tried and tested association. It's a healthy return to childhood that helps out today's kids as a bonus.

MUSIC BOX STEPS

The forgotten shooting place of an Oscar-winning 1932 Laurel and Hardy short

900 Vendome Street
Silverlake

Before the freeways, when Los Angeles was served by an ample (if flawed) public transportation system, the city's hills were a chutes-and-ladders maze of steep staircases and byways – many of which are still totally accessible. Some are more famous than others.

The Music Box Steps, in Silverlake, earned their name from an early star turn in *The Music Box*, an Oscar-winning, 1932 Laurel and Hardy short in which the two comedians carry and drop a piano up the steep, 133 steps between Vendome Street and Descanso Drive.

A remake of the lost 1927 Laurel and Hardy short called *Hats Off* (which, incidentally, used the exact same staircase), *The Music Box* is one of the comedy duo's early sound films – a stone-cold slapstick classic that completely holds up.

And, nearly a century later, the most remarkable thing about The Music Box Steps today is just how totally unremarkable they are – a simple concrete corridor with a small plaque on one of the lower stairs. Like many of this city's celluloid ghosts, it's a mundane thing aptly framed, caught on film, and preserved for the ages.

The Hidden Steps, an institution for all LA sporty types

While some flights of steps, such as the Music Box Staircase, have become tangible Hollywood icons, our favorite LA secret steps are those of the High Tower Elevator (see page 80), which offer an incredible panorama and sensation of being alone in the world. Sometimes you just need to take a walk to discover a whole series of steps leading to the surrounding hills. Search out your favorite walks: from Silverlake to Pacific Palisades, from Culver City to Beachwood Canyon, from El Sereno to Echo Park, through downtown or Santa Monica, there are plenty of options for those who love hiking, cardio exercises, or urban exploration generally. Morning and evening, a lot of highly motivated sporty types gather at various points along the outside staircase, all over the city, to run up and down -- at full tilt. These makeshift workout sites are sometimes difficult to find, obscured by overhanging vegetation, but they're worth all the effort: climbing them can often bring a sweet reward like a one-off viewpoint. Grab your sneakers!

MEMORIAL PLAQUES TO "ROOM 8" THE CAT

(22)

Feline myth-maker, adopted by schoolkids over 16 years!

Elysian Heights Elementary School
1562 Baxter Street
elysian-lausd-ca.schoolloop.com/room8
Always visible from the street

If this story of the elementary school adopting a stray cat might have been trivial, it has become awe-inspiring – a myth only LA could produce.

While the lovable feline has been dead since the 1970s, he still generates a cult following in this quiet corner of Echo Park, a residential

area that has shot upscale in recent years.

It's the story of a fat gray tomcat who, from 1952 to 1968, made himself at home within the walls of Elysian Heights Elementary School, now decorated with plaques, designs, and mosaics in his honor. Even the school website keeps a dedicated page.

When he arrived in the famous Room 8 in 1952, Room 8 (a play on "roommate") was an ordinary stray cat, who soon grew attached to the students and teachers. The fidelity and regularity over the long school years of this cat made an impression. He was capable of spending the summer wandering around (just like the students) before returning at the start of the year to nap on the teacher's desk while the kids recited the early morning national anthem.

Sixteen years passed, during which he earned the right to a children's book telling his story (*A Cat Named Room 8*), an eponymous song (by acoustic guitarist Leo Kottke), a documentary (*Big Cat, Little Cat*), and, above all, hundreds of letters sent to the school daily, which were sometimes used as the basis of a student writing exercise. The letters were a response to the articles and TV reports in the main US media: after each vacation journalists eagerly awaited the cat's return, cameras at the ready. When Room 8 died, the *Los Angeles Times* even published a quarter-page obituary, joining the litany of tributes from the American press.

The craze has obviously lapsed nowadays, except among internet geeks. Students and teachers are familiar with the mythology surrounding their school, but you're unlikely to see many tourists outside. On the other hand, be respectful if you're framing a few photos of the floor and walls, but don't venture inside and just take a discreet glance at the original plaques in passing, to avoid disrupting the smooth running of the school.

For added peace of mind and to ensure nobody is disturbed, Room 8's grave is located at Los Angeles Pet Memorial Park, several miles away. It offers an opportunity to stroll around the very chic town of Calabasas, north-east of Malibu.

Los Angeles Pet Memorial Park & Crematory
5068 North Old Scandia Lane, Calabasas
(818) 591-7037 – lapetcemetery.com
Monday, Tuesday, Thursday, Friday, Saturday, 8am–4:30pm

FACES OF ELYSIAN VALLEY

The first roundabout in LA is in a league of its own

501 North San Fernando Road
https://greenmeme.com
Always visible from the road

The art and design studio Greenmeme is behind some of the city's most creative urban installations (notably *Concrete Wallpaper* along 405 Freeway at Sepulveda Pass Westwood, or *Hyperion Son of Uranus* at the Environmental Learning Center of a wastewater treatment plant). In 2017 nine faces carved from an egg-shaped block of granite were erected near Dodger Stadium, with the constant concern of preserving the surrounding landscape.

Designed by Freya Bardell and Brian Howe, the first roundabout in LA is a public artwork depicting the faces of some of the unknown locals who have shaped the city (scanning workshops were set up to capture their features). It was planned as a gateway to the communities that surround it, such as Elysian Valley, Cypress Park, and Lincoln Heights. But this installation is primarily a stormwater detention site that traps water coming from the adjacent Riverside Drive Bridge.

The rainwater is retained in the outer circle by permeable pavers, also decorated with faces (the stones are offcuts from the vertical sculptures), while local waterwise plants have been carefully chosen to harmonize the group. Over 200 people contributed to this municipal project, which took seven years to develop. A model of "consciously green" urban art.

ADVENTURERS' CLUB OF LOS ANGELES MEETING ROOM

(24)

Old-fashioned exploration and exotic artifacts

Adventurers' Club of Los Angeles
2433 North Broadway
(323) 223-3948
adventurersclub.org
Weekly events, conferences and dinners open to non-members, by reservation only, from 6pm to 9:30pm most Thursdays (note that some evenings are reserved for club members – check website before each event)
Dress code: "business casual"

Tucked away in an unmistakable Lincoln Heights shopping mall, above a drugstore next to which a narrow staircase casts a yellowish light, this "Adventurers' Club" does not at first inspire confidence. And yet,once through the door, we're transported to a setting that looks as if it was taken from Indiana Jones' most feverish dreams.

Judge for yourself: a kayak weathered by the elements, a stuffed polar bear, pre-Columbian pottery, World War II helmets, strongboxes, flags, an authentic mammoth skeleton, a monkey's head, a (shrunken) human head from an Amazonian ritual ... The artifacts that decorate this otherwise banal meeting room are far from that.

Even the members, mostly gentlemen of a venerable age who boast of having "climbed Everest without oxygen," "surfed in the Arctic," "fought in the War," or "fished for eel on six continents," seem to come from a bygone era of old-style explorers, with anecdotes worthy of Jules Verne. Whether they teach rather old-fashioned self-defense or host

writers for a lengthy discussion, their vision of adventure has a certain ... gloss.

Back in 1922, Captain John Roulac brought together this strange group of advisers in search of sporting, human, and anthropological exploits. Among the most illustrious members were US President Teddy Roosevelt, astronaut Buzz Aldrin, and movie director James Cameron. Big names in terrestrial and space exploration, archaeologists and other scientists, but also anonymous folk who travel off the beaten track: all love to tell their stories and listen to others, whether adventurers or public speakers, every Thursday evening.

With around a hundred members (up to 1,000 in its heyday), the club still does not accept contributions from women, except on "Open Nights." To compensate, non-members, women and men, are welcome (reservation only).

This resolutely old-school club, bordering on bad taste with its rhino and howler monkey trophies on the walls, is a valuable sociological experience and museum of adventure. The good points are that these gentlemen from a time that the under-20s may not recognize, know how to make you welcome: their anecdotes are juicy, the bar well stocked and the dining accessible.

UCLA's impressive collection of meteorites

UCLA Meteorite Collection
Room 3697, Geology Building
595 Charles E. Young Drive East
meteorites.ucla.edu
Monday–Friday, 9am–4pm

Another range of fascinating artifacts awaits the visitor at UCLA (University of California Los Angeles) on the Westwood campus. In Room 3697, the geology department houses the second-largest collection of meteorites in the United States.

This all started when William Andrews Clark (see page 94) donated to the university a 353-pound fragment of the Canyon Diablo fireball, which crashed to Earth 49,000 years ago.

Since then, the university has assembled 2,400 samples that can be seen on site.

From Los Feliz to Malibu

1. GRIFFITH PARK ABANDONED ZOO — 64
2. THE ORIGINAL "BATCAVE" OF BRONSON CANYON — 66
3. SHAKESPEARE BRIDGE — 68
4. "HAPPY FOOT / SAD FOOT" SIGN AT SILVERLAKE — 70
5. HOLLYHOCK HOUSE — 72
6. CHARLES BUKOWSKI'S BUNGALOW — 74
7. CONSTANCE AND CARL BIGSBY'S "MISSILE GRAVE" — 76
8. MUSEUM OF DEATH — 78
9. HIGH TOWER ELEVATOR ASSOCIATION — 80
10. MAGIC CASTLE — 82
11. MUHAMMAD ALI'S STAR — 84
12. HAMBURGER MARY'S BINGO — 86
13. GILMORE GAS STATION AT FARMERS MARKET — 88
14. BERLIN WALL SEGMENTS — 90
15. WARNER MURAL IN WILSHIRE BOULEVARD SYNAGOGUE — 92
16. WILLIAMS ANDREWS CLARK MEMORIAL LIBRARY — 94

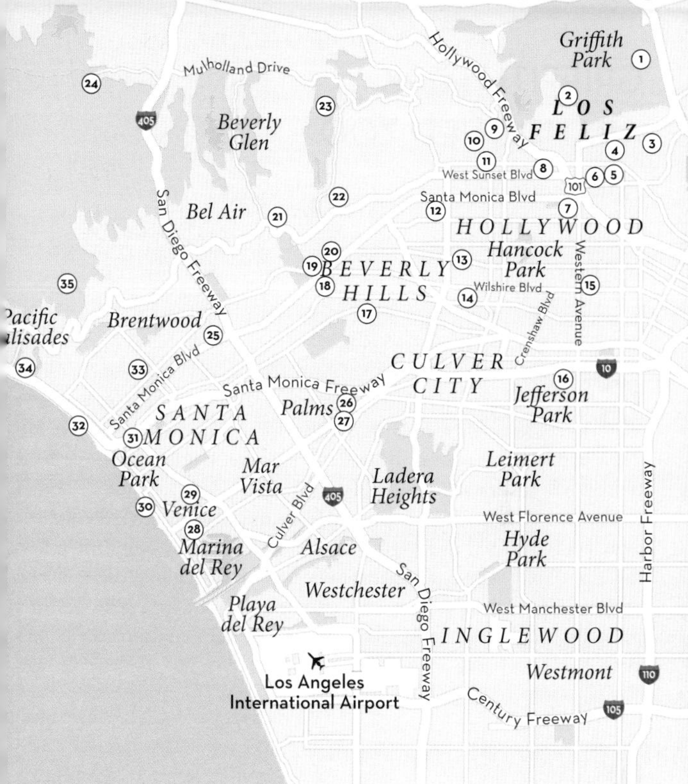

17 CARDIFF TOWER 96
18 CELLULOID MONUMENT 98
19 "WITCH'S HOUSE" 100
20 O'NEILL HOUSE 102
21 FREDERICK R. WEISMAN ART FOUNDATION 104
22 MONTHLY OPEN DAY AT GREYSTONE MANSION 106
23 PLAQUE MARKING THE EXACT CENTER OF THE CITY 108
24 HIKE ON THE LA-96C ANTI-MISSILE DEFENSE SITE 110
25 SACRED WATER SOURCE OF THE TONGVA 112
26 CLAY SCULPTURES AT THE BHAGAVAD-GITA MUSEUM 114
27 MUSEUM OF JURASSIC TECHNOLOGY 116
28 BIG LEBOWSKI APARTMENT 118
29 THE MOSAIC TILE HOUSE 120
30 VENICE BEACH RAINBOW LIFEGUARD STATION 122
31 THE "OFFICIAL" TERMINUS OF ROUTE 66 124
32 GRUNION RUN 126
33 FRANK GEHRY RESIDENCE 128
34 EAMES HOUSE 130
35 HIKING AT MURPHY RANCH 132
36 ABANDONED SETS FROM M*A*S*H 134

GRIFFITH PARK ABANDONED ZOO

①

How about a picnic in the tiger's cage?

4730 Crystal Springs Drive
laparks.org
(323) 644-2050
5am–10:30pm
Metro stop: Red Line Vermont / Sunset

Griffith Park has many hidden nooks and crannies, places you may never see and if you do, you might forget how to find them again. There are roads that seem to lead to nowhere, hidden caves, gardens, pine groves and an abandoned zoo.

About two miles down the road from the Los Angeles Zoo, hidden away behind an old merry-go-round and tucked away in a little valley, there is a lovely grassy area surrounded by empty animal cages. It's an imaginative place for a picnic, an adventurous spot for a hike, and the perfect setting to see Shakespeare in the Park on a midsummer night's eve.

Many years ago, it was a zoo with exotic animals from around the world. Some came from movie sets, early pioneer life, or private collections, and some from its predecessor, the Eastlake Zoo that closed its gates when the Griffith Park Zoo opened in 1912.

It began as a rather small zoo with only 15 animals when it took over the former property of Griffith J. Griffith's ostrich farm. In the 1930s, the zoo was greatly expanded as part of the Works Progress Administration under Franklin Delano Roosevelt. In 1966, all the animals were transferred to the new Los Angeles Zoo across from the Gene Autry Museum.

Today, one can hike, walk, climb, play and dine inside what remains of the lion, tiger and bear cages as if spending the day on a movie set. Perhaps you might see the ghost of Johnny Weissmuller or George the MGM lion.

No matter what you choose to do while visiting the old Griffith Park Zoo, you'll be left with the haunted feeling of another time whether in your imagination or from a movie you might have seen since this is a frequently used film and television location for shows like *Starsky and Hutch*, *ChiPs*, *Wonder Woman*, and *Police Academy 2*.

THE ORIGINAL "BATCAVE" OF BRONSON CANYON

②

Walk (without Batmobile) up to Batman's secret cave

3200 Canyon Drive
+1 (818) 243-1145 (Los Angeles Department of Recreation and Parks, Parks and Recreation Office)
laparks.org/park/bronson-canyon
Daily 5am–10:30pm

This guide won't give you the best routes up to the iconic HOLLYWOOD sign perched on the hill, as the various hiking trails, some steeper than others, are all described in any tourist guidebook.

But the sight of the huge white letters erected in 1923 is always worthwhile, whether you're out walking in Griffith Park or around the highest points of the city. And what could be more rewarding than enjoying this unique view as you emerge from ... Batman's secret cave!

In the first installment of Batman adventures made for early 1960s television, the writers had fun incorporating scenes in his legendary den, based on some of the comic strips. This ultramodern crime lab – supposedly in the basement of the Wayne family mansion – was only accessible by operating hidden levers. During the chases involving the Batmobile, his tricked-out car, the characters left the Batcave through a concealed gap in the rockface in hot pursuit of the bad guys.

As the series obviously was shot in LA, Griffith Park's natural setting was used as the fictitious Gotham City. Southwest of the park, leave your car at 3200 Canyon Drive before tackling the relatively easy climb of Bronson Canyon. In less than 15 minutes this will take you to the cave entrance, now open and accessible to hikers. Be like Batman and leave the tunnel (excavated in the early 20th century and still regularly used for filming), but instead of giving chase, head left after the second small cave for a breathtaking view of the HOLLYWOOD sign. The circuit only takes half an hour, but allow a good hour if you want to take photos.

Further north, the Brush Canyon Trail takes you to the HOLLYWOOD letters in less than an hour, which could make a perfect double trip – but don't say we told you about it.
A useful tip for any hike beyond the city: in the early morning or at nightfall watch out for rattlesnakes (cover your legs and keep your eyes peeled)!

SHAKESPEARE BRIDGE

③

One of the most romantic sites in Los Angeles

4001 Franklin Avenue
Bridge starts at St George Street
+1 (323) 908-6078
franklinhills.org

This short road bridge, on the National Register of Historic Places since 1974, was built in 1926 and reinforced in 1998 following the Northridge earthquake (1994). It's one of the most romantic sites in Los Angeles.

Not only does the bridge cross a little valley in the heart of Los Feliz, it also shelters a tiny garden between the piers (entrance at 1900 Monon Street). Although the Franklin Hills community residents include some well-known movie stars, they've nothing to do with Shakespeare and are very active in preserving the authenticity of their corner of the historic neighborhood. Since renovation, the bridge, 260 feet long and 30 feet wide, is regularly garlanded with lights by the Franklin Hills Residents Association.

Originally this little gem cost a mammoth $60,000, but close neighbors and onlookers were not too happy with the results of architect J.C. Wright's work. A topical article in the *Los Angeles Times* stated, "such a bridge will [have] no interest for the public." Ironically, it's been the darling of the neighborhood since. Pedestrian access to the ravine, through which a stream known as "Arroyo de la Sacatela" once ran, is a series of stairways dating from the same era as the concrete bridge. Not many drivers take the trouble to admire its Gothic spires as the sidewalk is narrow, but you can park a few minutes at the east entrance to check it out.

You won't want to spend the day, but the bridge is certainly a spectacular photo stop on the way to many of the city's don't-miss attractions, including Walt Disney's first house (2495 Lyric Avenue), Hollyhock House in Barnsdall Park (4800 Hollywood Boulevard, see page 72) and the ABC Prospect Studios (4151 Prospect Avenue), where countless TV shows have been made since the 1950s – a far cry from the verses recited by Shakespearean players back in the day.

④

"HAPPY FOOT / SAD FOOT" SIGN AT SILVERLAKE

Image of a foot with unsuspected powers

Previous location: 2711 West Sunset Boulevard
Present location: 1770 North Vermont Avenue

It was one of the most recognizable highlights of super-cool Silverlake. Who'd have thought that this rotating sign, like an unflappable weather vane, would have such cult status? And yet, the double-sided sign of a local podiatrist, with a cartoon foot in great shape on one side, and an injured foot on crutches on the other (with the slogan "Foot Clinic" and phone number), became a neighborhood symbol in the city's arty circles over the years.

The celebrated sign, featured in a 2007 novel set locally (Jonathan Lethem's *You Don't Love Me Yet*), served as the main character's compass for crucial decisions – the foot was treated as an all-powerful god. For musicians Beck and Eels, it was more of an oracle, as both claimed it had prophetic qualities when they lived at Silverlake.

"Will your day be a disaster or a success? Ask the foot." Depending on the side that first showed itself on leaving the house, you learned your fate. David Foster Wallace also conjured up the foot in his novel *The Pale King*. And it starred in a fantastic video clip from electropop band YACHT. The neighborhood-branding mode went into overdrive as only Americans can when they dubbed it HaFo / SaFo.

So imagine the consternation when, in 2019, Dr Lim decided to shut up shop and take down his spinning sign.

What would become of the unofficial localicon? The suspense dragged on for months. Finally, late in the year, Bill Wyatt, owner of Y-Que Trading Post (in nearby Los Feliz) and a great fan of the foot, bought the sign as it was about to be demolished and maneuvered it into his clothing store.

Since then, there's been daily "foot traffic" as a handful of insiders drop in to pay their respects to the two-sided icon.

Silverlake neighborhood on foot

From Sunset Junction to Echo Park Lake, via Silverlake Reservoir in one direction and Sunset Boulevard on the way back, the loop takes 1 hour 40 minutes.
Add a tour of said lake, do lunch, a spot of shopping – it's an ideal way to discover hipster LA in half a day.
Now you can add a trip to the Los Felix store to admire the relocated Happy Foot / Sad Foot.

HOLLYHOCK HOUSE

⑤

Frank Lloyd Wright's unloved masterpiece

Barnsdall Art Park
4800 Hollywood Boulevard
+1 (213) 626-1901
barnsdall.org
Park open daily 6am–10pm
Junior Art Center: Monday to Friday 10am–6pm, Saturday 10am–4pm
Art gallery: Thursday to Sunday 12 noon–5pm
House tours: Thursday to Sunday 11am–4pm
Last tickets sold daily at 3:30pm

Hollyhock House, an eccentric creation from Frank Lloyd Wright's early career when his work was not yet widely celebrated, was unloved before reverting to one of LA's hidden architectural gems.

Unloved by the owner, oil heiress Aline Barnsdall who rarely stayed in the house, it was left to the city in 1927 along with the park that now bears her name.

Unloved by the architect himself, who was experimenting with an intermediate concept before his "Prairie School" masterpieces (such as the Fallingwater residence in Pennsylvania) and his unsurpassable Solomon R. Guggenheim Museum in New York City, the carved concrete façades are reminiscent of Mayan temples and traditional Japanese homes.

This construction technique, using textured concrete blocks, is at the crossroads between the few large buildings commissioned by some municipality or other and the hymns to nature that the American master later designed.

Seen from a modern perspective, the house is gorgeous. The style, which came to be known as "California Romanza," blends cast concrete, ornate pillars, Art Nouveau and modernist elements, a half-covered central fountain, walkways like miniature bridges spanning a canal, and a splendid chimney with egypto-Bauhaus bas-reliefs. This marvelous mix demands a tour of the interior, because the exterior with its massive Masonic temple aspect may seem austere, despite the welcoming outlines of Barnsdall Park hillside and the spectacular view. Note that the park also houses a cinema, art gallery, and community arts center.

Frank Lloyd Wright's eldest son, Lloyd Wright, who oversaw the construction of the outbuildings, is also the main architect of the other Mayan-revival house in Los Feliz district, located a few hundred yards away. It soon became legendary, for good reason: with its entrance shaped like a shark's gaping jaws, John Sowden house at 5121 Franklin Avenue was the scene in 1947 of one of the city's most notorious murders — that of Elizabeth Short, better known as the "Black Dahlia."

© Teemu008 from Palatine, Illinois

CHARLES BUKOWSKI'S BUNGALOW

6

Once home of the iconic writer, now a historic monument

5124 De Longpre Avenue
Closed to the public
Metro: Red Line, Vermont / Sunset stop

Thanks to the combined efforts of Lauren Everett and Richard Schave, the modest bungalow that American writer Charles Bukowski rented at 5124 De Longpre Avenue for nearly a decade was given a last-minute reprieve from demolition.

It was a victory for fans of *Post Office*, his first novel, written here in 21 days and published in 1971 in the United States, after years spent composing short stories and poetry without much success.

Everett and Schave, photographer and historian by trade (Schave also founded a business running unconventional bus tours of the city known as "Esotouric"), had led a fervent campaign against aggressive real estate developers aiming to convert the few bungalows on the avenue into modern buildings. Though this little house is nothing special, in 2008 it was listed on the National Register of Historic Places. In this way the Los Angeles Cultural Heritage Commission saves some 40 monuments per year, whether for their great architectural value or, as here, for their contribution to the history of the city. The letters perched on the hillside spelling out Hollywood, Watts Towers in South Los Angeles, and the Shrine Auditorium at the University of Southern California are among the family of LA monuments saved "forever" from the ravages of time – or demolition.

"The neighborhood has remained working class, with a community of Russians, Armenians, Slavs who arrived in the 1960s and 1970s," Richard Schave told the press at the time of the Bukowski house rescue. "Around the corner, Pink Elephant Liquors, the writer's favorite store, is still there. It was on De Longpre Avenue that his work exploded on the world. This place was the booster that marked the rest of his life." From this pivotal era, through the voice of its founder John Martin, Black Sparrow Press became Bukowski's legendary publisher.

A plaque in the street now commemorates this victory of art over profit, and though the bungalow is private you can still see it clearly from outside. And maybe you could ask the current tenants for permission to snap a souvenir photo.

CONSTANCE AND CARL BIGSBY'S ⑦ "MISSILE GRAVE"

"Too bad ... we had fun"

Hollywood Forever Cemetery
6000 Santa Monica Boulevard
+1 (323) 469-1181
hollywoodforever.com
Monday–Friday 8:30am–5pm, Saturday and Sunday until 4:30pm
Admission free

Hollywood Forever Cemetery, one of the country's most iconic, is home to an impressive number of celebrities. Many stars of American television, theater, and cinema are buried in this beautiful green setting of 60 acres, bordered by palm trees and close to the Paramount studios (one probably explains the other). Not content just as *the place to be* for the deceased, since the early 2000s the cemetery has managed to renew its appeal to the living, notably by hosting parties, film screenings, and outdoor concerts every summer.

But this attractive patch of land is also the last resting place of complete strangers, who sometimes exceed the limits of good taste, romance, decency or whimsy when purchasing their tombstone.

Such as that of graphic artist Carl Bigsby and his wife, Constance. Their plot in central section 13 (lot 521), is the base of a life-size replica of the Atlas-B missile, which on December 18, 1958, sent into orbit the first communications satellite in history. This successful launch set the United States back on the path to successful space conquest, after initially falling behind Sputnik, the Soviet orbital launcher used successfully the year before.

Carl Bigsby, who died on May 3, 1959, considered himself – not without some humor – as a graphic design "pioneer," just like the decisive Atlas mission. "The Atlas, pioneer in space, symbolizes the lifetime activities of Carl Morgan Bigsby, a recognized leader in many phases of the graphic arts, he too was a pioneer," reads his droll epitaph, surmounted by a super statue of the missile: a type of tombstone not seen every day.

The epitaph of Constance Bigsby, who died many years later in 2000, doesn't even mention her date of death. Just above the year of birth (1914) is engraved a phrase that every bon vivant would like to make their own: "Too bad ... we had fun." The couple obviously knew how to savor life without taking themselves too seriously. Their offbeat tribute to the heroes of the space conquest is at the same time poetic, grandiose, and facetious. A godsend for those who love abandoned unusual finds and aren't interested in the graves of Marilyn Monroe or Mickey Rooney.

MUSEUM OF DEATH

⑧

"One or two visitors faint every week"

Museum of Death
6031 Hollywood Boulevard
+1 (323) 466-8011
museumofdeath.net
Sunday to Thursday 10am–8pm, Friday 10am–9pm, Saturday 10am–10pm
Metro: Red Line, Hollywood & Vine stop

The photos and descriptions can be very graphic, and some find that too gory." Better to be warned.

The first room sets the tone: while still totally accessible even to a sensitive audience, it's dedicated to the face of the serial killer, a theme embedded deep in the American psyche. But the museum's two founders, Cathee Shultz and J.D. Healy, also have sourced European artifacts such as the mummified head of Henri Désiré Landru, the French crook turned murderer (between 1915 and 1919 he killed 10 women and conned around 300 more).

Around him are numerous drawings, objects and correspondence between known serial killers (John Wayne Gacy, Ted Bundy, Richard Ramirez) and their family or "fans," accompanied by a mockup of an electric chair. The museum founders have so far failed to procure the real thing.

After the rooms describing the techniques used by funeral directors over the years, antiquities from various morgues around the world and the skeletons of dogs and giraffes, among other oddities, the first photos of autopsies take their place in this danse macabre. But, according to the owners (who opened a New Orleans branch in 2015), it's meant "to make you happy to be alive."

The horror level of these images gradually rises, but it's so well done that you get used to seeing severed heads, photos of crime scenes and road accidents or killers posing with their dismembered victims. Happily the museum doesn't go in for sensationalism, aiming to educate rather than shock.

Witness the relatively sober room dedicated to Charles Manson and his murderous "family." Or another recounting the evils of Jeffrey Dahmer, which sticks to the facts even though the detailed descriptions send shivers up your spine. After that, photos of suicides seem quite touching.

The display of the deceased and famous (and their faithful four-legged friends – some stuffed specimens are displayed) relieves the tension before you exit through the souvenir shop, where skull-printed tees begin to feel civilized.

HIGH TOWER ELEVATOR ASSOCIATION

⑨

A private community lift for local residents

2178 High Tower Drive
Tower can be seen from the street

Attention, great favorite! A neighborhood gem that you could only find in LA, with a breathtaking panoramic view, a most unusual building, all popular with ... hardly anybody.

Only local residents can access this quaint, five-story tower resembling a lighthouse in the Hollywood Heights neighborhood (for a monthly fee of around $50, the happy owners and tenants of nearby

homes can use the private community lift inside, the only one west of the Mississippi). The streets and steps are, of course, public.

From Highland Avenue, walk through Highland Camrose Park before taking the stairway to Alta Loma Terrace. Then a series of steps (not always connected to each other) surround the attractive tower from all angles.

Along the walk, bougainvillea, palm trees, and eminently European architecture are all-enveloping. The often overwhelming calm is disturbed only by birdsong, despite the Hollywood Walk of Fame down below on one side and the vibrant Hollywood Bowl on the other. At sunset, the magnificent light offers a spectacular setting for the city, whose silhouette can be seen right up to the downtown foothills.

Although the tower, modeled after some Italian bell tower, was erected almost a century ago to spare hill dwellers from wearing themselves out on their way home, the apartments and houses are more reminiscent of Hollywood's heyday between 1930 and 1950. It's a time capsule, then, whose tranquility is such a contrast to the hustle and bustle of the surrounding hills and stairways that discovering it is a true delight.

Tip: if you're too broke to take in a concert at the Bowl, you can still join the throngs that rush to the iconic amphitheater every summer evening, with picnicbasket, and branch left just before the entrance, to eat out in the hills. A few benches are waiting at the top.

Hidden stairs that became Hollywood stars

While our favorite secret stairs are at the High Tower Elevator (see above), they are far from the only ones. From Silverlake to Pacific Palisades, Culver City to Beachwood Canyon, El Sereno to Echo Park, downtown and Santa Monica, there's plenty of options for hiking and cardio junkies.

As proof, morning and evening, some seasoned sporty types gather around such stairs all over LA. The stairs are sometimes difficult to flush out, hidden by dense greenery, but some have morphed into Hollywood stars, like the Music Box Staircase (935 Vendome Avenue, Silverlake), which Laurel and Hardy used in 1932 for an Oscar-winning short, *The Music Box.*

MAGIC CASTLE

A really unique experience

7001 Franklin Avenue
+1 (323) 851-3313
magiccastle.com
Daily 5pm–2am; brunches on weekends 10am–3pm
Metro: Red Line, Hollywood / Highland stop

Although strictly speaking the Magic Castle is no secret, unashamedly flaunting its kitsch frontage and clearly visible from Franklin Avenue, between the route that leads to Hollywood Bowl and

the overcrowded Walk of Fame (the legendary stars set in the sidewalks are tourist magnets), it's perhaps the most unusual site in this guide.

This "secret," ineffectively kept since 1963, has the distinction of being an exclusive and very chic private club that features a restaurant, bar, school, and temple devoted to all kinds of magic.

Unfortunately (or fortunately, maybe) it's not easy to get accepted to spend an evening there: it's no good just knocking on the door in your party clothes.

Five options are available to curious visitors: being a club member (only 5,000 professionals worldwide can lay claim to this); knowing an employee (magicians included); taking classes at the Academy of Magical Arts; or being invited by a student. The final option is to stay at the Magic Castle Hotel, an upgraded and surprisingly modern motel just steps from the "real" Gothic castle. But that would be a great loss in mystery and charm.

Once the door – guarded by a carved owl – swings open at the recitation of a magic formula, the sight is quite enchanting: a labyrinth of alcoves, intimate bars, a large dining room upstairs, a phantom pianist who responds to the spoken word and plays your favorite standards. Everywhere, up flights of stairs or along narrow corridors, are little theaters, upstairs, downstairs, in the basement, some with 10 seats, others with 100, where masters of their art follow one another on stage from 5pm to 2am. A sort of mini Las Vegas of magic, fewer casinos and more intimacy, with a haunted castle feel. A truly unique experience.

Watch out: the Magic Castle has maybe the most stringent dress code in Los Angeles (apart from the Oscars ceremony): evening gowns for women; suit, tie, and dress shoes for men.

In the very casual LA, where execs often come to work in Bermuda shorts, this rarity needs highlighting.

Another warning if you manage to book: as the bartenders are so talented and adorable (some also do magic tricks), content yourself with a drink: the restaurant, expensive, can freely be passed over.

MUHAMMAD ALI'S STAR

The only Hollywood star you can't walk over

6801 Hollywood Boulevard
walkoffame.com
Metro: Red Line, Hollywood / Highland

It was in 2002 that the planet's best-known boxer, who was born Cassius Clay in 1942 and died in 2016, was honored with a star on the celebrated Walk of Fame, those few blocks of the Hollywood district where the names of the best-known stage and screen idols are inscribed.

It's true that athletes are only commemorated there if their performances had massive TV coverage or if they also contributed to the entertainment industry. The stars cover the following five categories only: Motion Picture, Television, Recording, Radio, and Live Performance.

So, for example, Magic Johnson is featured as the owner of a cinema chain after his career as a basketball player. The last category, Live Performance, was awarded to Muhammad Ali. A legend not content with placing the art of boxing at center stage, he "lived his life as if on the boards," according to the committee that hands out these accolades. But that's not the only incongruity linked to the siting of his star in the heart of this tourist magnet.

Although the very popular Walk of Fame attraction isn't really worth more than 10 minutes of your time on a first visit to LA, it's interesting to note that Ali's star is the only one mounted on a vertical surface – a discreet corner of the wall at the entrance to the Dolby Theatre. The boxer, who converted to Islam in 1964, had asked for special treatment so that nobody could walk on the name he shared with the Prophet. "I don't want the star trampled by people who've no respect for me," he told the press. So, he's the only celeb to have benefited from such a favor and thus attract more interest than the other 2,500.

Synchronized swimmers at the Dolby Theatre

Muhammad Ali and Magic Johnson aren't the only athletes around the Dolby Theatre.

Formerly known as the Kodak, the backdrop to the annual Academy Awards ceremony still bears one of the symbols of the silver screen and old movies: synchronized swimmers embedded in the black marble floor. To see them, climb the central staircase and look down towards the ground, below the skylight.

HAMBURGER MARY'S BINGO

(12)

Drag-queen bingo

8288 Santa Monica Boulevard, West Hollywood
+1 (323) 654-3800
bingoboyinc.com orhamburgermarys.com
Every Wednesday at 7pm and 9pm, every Sunday at 6pm and 8pm
Additional events on certain Thursday evenings and in different parts of the city
Entrance: $20 for 11 bingo grids; food and drinks optional; reservation highly recommended
Access: US-101 N, exit Sunset Boulevard

What's the name of the game?
– BINGO!
– And how do we play it?
– LOUD!"

She's a mixed-race drag queen with ultra-luscious curves and fuchsia makeup who screams into a microphone, and the delirious crowd at their tables responds by shouting even louder. Forget about traditional Sunday bingo, here the game is played to yells and applause, and each winner has to run around the room, the discarded rolled-up cards of disgruntled losers bouncing off their head. Five times a week, Jeffrey Bowman's colorful crew takes over Hamburger Mary's, an institution in West Hollywood, LA's gay district (in fact a full-fledged city, which in 1984 became the first homosexual majority municipality in the United States).

Far from being confined to the community, this experience has over the years become the favorite venue for a few faithful Angelenos, making it the city's longest-running biweekly charity event. No tourists here (for the moment), only locals of all ages who have come to have fun for a good cause, whether to help breast cancer research, support LGBT visibility, or finance a homeless shelter. The second time we went, a stray kitten rescue association run by very respectable elderly people was fund-raising. And the association's spokesperson didn't flinch at a gentle spanking with a BDSM leather paddle for a bingo false alert: this is the rule after a wrong call, and nobody gets away with it!

In this good-natured bazaar where the noise level drowns you, we elbow our way through to try the top-quality burgers and salads, decadent cocktails on the side. But you don't need to eat and drink to join in this madness, as long as you reserve a table and leave your prejudices at home, to take part in Bowman's original dream: simply to open up charity galas to the middle classes.

The bar-restaurant also has a branch at Long Beach (without bingo) and others across the United States, including one in San Francisco, a pioneer when it open in 1972, that has since become a pillar of the LGBT community and culture.

GILMORE GAS STATION AT FARMERS MARKET

⑬

Black gold revelation at dairy farm

6333 West 3rd Street
+1 (323) 933-9211
farmersmarketla.com
Daily 9am–9pm, except Sundays (10am–7pm)

Although The Grove, an open-air shopping mall, is far from authentic with its glitzy shops, faux-kitsch streetcar, and ubiquitous music, the adjacent Farmers Market is a vibrant foodie getaway, redolent with flavors from around the world.

The site, originally owned by Arthur Fremont Gilmore, was a dairy farm where a few neighboring farmers began to rent space once a week to sell their produce to the locals, as early as 1880. But in 1900, Gilmore, prospecting for water for his livestock, made a discovery that would transform his life – not to mention his bank account: oil! Goodbye farm and farmers, the Gilmore Oil Company was born.

In a booming region where development was centered on the automobile, oil was a significant and lasting windfall for the site owner. The income from his wells, then the most productive in California, was conspicuously spent on paving the dusty West Coast roads. Then, after selling his brand of black gold (with its roaring lion logo) to all the nearby gas stations, came the first automated station where customers could serve themselves. In a clever promotional detail, the pumps were transparent and patrons could see the precious liquid flowing through the pipes.

The success of Salt Lake Oil Field (the official name of the site, straddling several geologic faults), later exploited by family scion E.B. Gilmore, encouraged the owners to diversify: motor racing, baseball and American football teams (L.A. Bulldogs), movies, circuses ... before Farmers Market reappeared in 1934.

To commemorate these successful transitional years, a refurbished gas station now marks the boundary between the market and the mall. The dried-up wells were producing just 30 barrels of oil a day shortly before operations shut down, according to Texaco, the last owner.

Marilyn Monroe was voted Miss Cheesecake of the Year at the 1953 Farmers Market.

Gas station to Starbucks

Another station formerly owned by the Gilmore family has been converted to Starbucks Coffee, on the corner of Willoughby Avenue and Highland Avenue, in the Melrose neighborhood. That alone is worth the trip, as the preservation of the original structure is a great success.

BERLIN WALL SEGMENTS

(14)

The longest stretch of the Berlin Wall outside of Germany

5900 Wilshire Boulevard
+1 (310) 216-1600
wendemuseum.org/programs/wall-project

First, to emphasize how much these relics are worth visiting: the 10 "Berlin Wall segments," gathered in front of one of LA's most iconic museums, form the longest stretch of this sad symbol of the Cold War outside Germany.

Although they don't belong to the Los Angeles County Museum of Art (LACMA) just opposite, but to the Wende Museum based in Culver City, it would still be a pity to miss them, given their proximity to Museum Row.

The ten wall segments stand opposite artist Chris Burden's famous *Urban Light* (2008) assemblage sculpture of 1920s and 1930s street lamps, which draws thousands of selfie fans every day, and next to the food trucks where folks sustain themselves after viewing this impressive mastodon. They are covered with street art commissioned by the Wende

Museum in 2009 for the 20th anniversary of the fall of the Berlin Wall, as part of the aptly-named public art "Wall Project."

An irritated green bear, the faces of JFK and Ronald Reagan, a curious orange guy, Nelson Mandela, sparkling bubbles of color, graffiti worthy of the New York subway and even a geologic fault (San Andreas?) are just some of the almost cartoon-like motifs decorating the wall relics.

On the other side: Captain America watches, accompanied by two pregnant women, and pixaçãos, those stylized graffiti tags that arose in the febrile ambiance of São Paulo, Brazil.

Only the bear was already painted (by Berlin street artist Bimer) when the 40 ft (12 m) segments were transported to Southern California.

The other artists were selected to decorate the remaining segments after their installation on Wishire Boulevard: Thierry Noir, a Frenchman already long associated with the Berlin Wall (see page 150), muralist Kent Twitchell, Marie Astrid González and Farrah Karapetian for the front, West Berlin-facing side; Retna, D*Face and Herakut for the side that faced East Berlin and the former GDR (though in fact two walls and a militarized buffer zone separated the two Berlins at the time).

Today's visitors are free to move around on either side of the former separation without bothering about checkpoints.

WARNER MURAL IN WILSHIRE BOULEVARD SYNAGOGUE

⑮

Religious paintings funded by famous movie magnates

Wilshire Boulevard Temple
3663 Wilshire Blvd
wbtla.org
Visits by appointment

Wilshire Boulevard Temple, a synagogue attended by B'nai B'rith, LA's oldest Jewish community, is very easy to spot on the city's longest through street. Its immense neo-Byzantine dome, designed by A.M. Edelman, can be seen from a distance.

You can book a visit and check out in particular the immense biblical fresco stretching over 300 feet, enveloping the entire sanctuary. From Abraham to the "discovery" of America by Christopher Columbus, the various sections depict historical episodes and Jewish traditions.

The fresco was commissioned in 1929 by brothers Jack, Harry, and Albert Warner (the Warner Brothers) from artistic director Hugo Ballin, who used to work with them on movie sets. It was Rabbi Edgar Magnin, impressed by European cathedrals and Hollywood studio productions, who had the idea of these fascinating murals, donated by the Warner brothers in the late 1920s and renovated in 2013 with obsessive fidelity to the original work.

Beyond their incongruous connection with the world of cinema and its highfalutin' imagery, these paintings are also rare in the history of Judaism. The Torah prohibits biblical representations in temples (second of the Ten Commandments: "Thou shalt have no other Gods before me. Thou shalt not make unto thee any graven image, or any likeness that is in heaven above, or in the earth beneath, or in the waters under the earth").

At the time, the rabbi justified his choice this way: "The days when people could not venerate images are behind us. Synagogues are generally too cold, we need more warmth and mysticism." The daring gamble is a great success.

WILLIAMS ANDREWS CLARK MEMORIAL LIBRARY

16

One of the largest collections of rare books in the United States

UCLA
2520 Cimarron Street
+1 (310) 794-5155
clarklibrary.ucla.edu
Reading room: Monday to Friday, 9am–4:45pm
Guided tours by appointment only
CA-110 West, West Adams Boulevard exit

A luxurious British baroque setting, in the style British universities use to protect their precious books. "A brilliant sun irresistibly drawing scholars, students and lucky others into its orbit," according to journalist Clara Sturak, author of an essay on the charm of the place.

The William Andrews Clark Memorial Library of rare books, one of the 12 wings of the University of California Los Angeles (UCLA), is a well-hidden treasure, and arguably the least-visited of them all.

Attached to the Center of 17th- and 18th-Century Studies of the prestigious UCLA faculty, the collection includes magnificent first editions of Charles Dickens and Jean-Jacques Rousseau, hundreds of Oscar Wilde's unpublished letters, and the first bound copy of the complete works of Shakespeare.

"No matter how valuable the works, they're accessible to the public," says one of the site librarians, Scott Jacobs, who occasionally organizes private tours of small groups by appointment.

Although the noble and impassive ground-floor rooms evoke a scholarship fixed in the past, with their bronze (fireproof) shelves, it's in the basement, where all the works can be consulted, that the magic of literature comes into its own, despite the surveillance cameras. How can you not be affected by Wilde's feverish missives to Alfred Douglas, his lover? Or the original editions of poems by Edgar Allan Poe, whose fragile pages need to be delicately turned by the library staff? For some editions, you'll simply be shown how to handle the works in a precise and ordered way, sometimes wearing white gloves.

William Andrews Clark was heir to a family that made a fortune in Montana copper. A lawyer, he was also the founder of the Los Angeles Philharmonic Orchestra. In 1906, his interest in literature led to the purchase of land at West Adams to build a mansion, a huge library and a house for his servants. Having handed the property over to UCLA in 1926, only the library was still standing when he died eight years later. The house had been demolished and the domestic accommodation had been moved to another location. Today, with its 100,000 rare books, the building is "one of the most unique in the city," concludes Jacobs as he closes its wide doors.

CARDIFF TOWER

⑰

Trompe-l'œil oil wells

9101 Pico Boulevard

The City of Los Angeles sits on any number of oil wells, such as the bubbling tar ponds of the La Brea Tar Pits near LACMA, from which models of prehistoric animals emerge (with a museum nearby). But with the exception of these famous open wells, the city seems to be ashamed of them. In some neighborhoods, the massive structures are doing their best not to reveal their purpose, such as the tower in Pico-Robertson, a historically Jewish enclave in southern Beverly Hills that hides its game very well.

At 9101 Pico Boulevard, a tall building that could be mistaken for a temple has no windows. And for good reason: this is in fact a group of 40 oil wells with a trompe-l'oeil covering. This curious construction, built by Occidental Petroleum, is known as Cardiff Tower.

The first building of its kind in LA, it was opened in 1966 by then-mayor Sam Yorty, who cut the ribbon while declaring the structure "an outstanding contribution to urban beauty."

Not everyone agrees nowadays. For several years, residents have worried about the possible presence of toxic waste near their homes. The local rabbi is trying unsuccessfully to shut down the oil exploitation, which many locals don't even know about. He wishes Cardiff Tower a fate similar to that of Tower of Hope, the huge oil rig smack dab in the middle of Beverly Hills High School grounds. The rig, hidden behind a flowered canvas decorated by sick children from a nearby hospital, was shut down in 2017 when the Venoco company went bust – even after previously contributing several hundred thousand dollars annually to the authorities. The tower is now covered with a huge tarpaulin.

The Packard Well Site and the Beverly Center well are also part of this amazing family of deceptive black gold buildings in the LA heartlands.

Camouflaged offshore oil platforms

Also in Long Beach, four artificial islands that can be seen from the harbor seem to mimic a theme park -- or modern and colorful high-rise apartment blocks. Anyone who sees them won't be surprised to learn that they were designed by Joseph Linesch, the architect who helped build the first Disneyland. Nicknamed Astronaut Islands, they've been the only camouflaged offshore oil platforms in the country since 1965.

CELLULOID MONUMENT

A group that fought for the independence of their city

352 South Beverly Drive, Beverly Hills
Always visible from nearby streets

This strange commemorative statue 22 feet high, a marble and bronze spiral evoking a ribbon of celluloid film surmounting depictions of the movie stars who have shaped the face of LA for decades, could pass for yet another example of the city paying homage to the seventh art. However, it has a much more political history and, ironically, tells the story of a rebellion. Erected in 1960, the monument is actually a tribute to the efforts of those who fought to preserve the independence of Beverly Hills from its sprawling neighbor.

Although the "City of Stars" became independent in 1914, it could have lost this status and been swallowed up by the megalopolis barely a decade later, when a proposal was made for LA to supply Beverly Hills with clean water — a game changer in California. Although part of Los Angeles County, the wealthy enclave has its own mayor and administration (just like West Hollywood). In 1923, most of the residents, including eight celebrities who had moved into these famed hills by the turn of the 20th century, campaigned for a vote against possible annexation. They emerged victorious.

At the convergence of South Beverly Drive, Olympic Boulevard, and South Beverwil Drive, the octagonal statue, discreet despite its size (chances are you'll drive by and miss it), shows Rudolph Valentino, Will Rogers, Mary Pickford, Harold Lloyd, Fred Niblo, Tom Mix, Douglas Fairbanks, and Conrad Nagle, all in costume. Below each figure is an inscription naming their most iconic role.

"WITCH'S HOUSE"

European architecture idealized by Hollywood

Spadena House (also known as the "Witch's House")
516 Walden Drive, Beverly Hills
Private property

The post-war years of the 1920s, the rapid expansion of the movie industry, the industrial era running out of steam and the fascination for different trends, typically European, gave rise to the Storybook or fairytale style of architecture. These houses, although rather a mismatch with postmodern LA decor, easy to stumble across on Californian architectural tours, are just a "Disneyfied" Hollywood version of common trends in parts of Europe where the medieval style made a comeback at the end of the 18th century.

As Arrol Gellner explains in his book on this building trend, *Storybook Style*, the Great War exposed many young Americans to Europe for the first time, and "it is all but certain that the quaint rural architecture of Flanders, France, and Germany, so different from that of the United States, would remain firmly fixed in every soldier's mind ..." Passed through the mill of architects and art directors used to working on film sets, this idealized vision produced quirky shapes, steeply sloping roofs, tiny stained-glass windows and crooked shutters, fireplaces straight out of the Brothers Grimm and intentionally overgrown gardens.

The best known of these art directors was Harry Oliver, who designed Spadena House (named after the first private owners) in 1921, originally for studio offices and dressing rooms. Although it has undergone many renovations over the years, especially inside, the disconcerting structure and moat-like pond make a delightfully anachronistic curiosity. But the house is still private property, so view it (and take photos) from the street.

Other Storybook buildings

These odd thatched cottages can still be rented or owned, despite their movie-set decor.

At 1330 North Formosa Avenue, Charlie Chaplin had a group of four houses built for rental in 1923 (Judy Garland and Douglas Fairbanks were among the stars who lived there).

Walt Disney was inspired by the style of the Tam O'Shanter restaurant (2980 Los Feliz Boulevard), still open for business.

And at Silverlake, 2900 Griffith Park Boulevard, is a group of eight thatched cottages thought to have influenced the set designers for *Snow White and the Seven Dwarfs*, released in 1937.

Today, in an ironic reversal of references, this complex (which appears notably in David Lynch's 2001 Gothic fantasy *Mulholland Drive*), is called "Snow White Cottages."

O'NEILL HOUSE

Beverly Hills tribute to Gaudí

507 North Rodeo Drive
View from the street

In a country with few legal barriers to construction, Los Angeles has pushed the lack of architectural regulations to the limit, exacerbated by vast fortunes able to realize the craziest urban visions.

The diverse styles range from Mid-Century Modern to Brutalism, through Storybook and Greco-Roman with kitsch touches. Beverly

Hills wins hands down in this contest for originality at all costs. The most remarkable creation has to be the O'Neill House, on famed Rodeo Drive, where celebrities and wealthy individuals come from all over the world to satisfy their appetite for upscale shopping in the shade of the palm trees.

Before the highway near Wilshire Boulevard grows steep and winding, like a miniaturized (and idealized) version of Paris complete with glitzy shops, further north, along immaculate alleyways, is Rodeo Drive. It's a near-normal road and one way into Beverly Flats – a multi-million-dollar neighborhood where each house is more improbable than the last. The first, at the corner of Park Way, is typical.

The Gaudí-inspired Art Nouveau structure has almost no right angles, just repetitive undulating and asymmetric curves. Yet its concrete overcoat hides a rather more traditional original construction.

Don O'Neill, the owner, was an art dealer obsessed by Catalan architect Antoni Gaudí. He and his wife, Sandy O'Neill, wanted to give their buildings a touch of Gaudí's crazy modernism in a "renovation" project that, over the years, took in the whole property. Unfortunately, just like the visionary architect, he would never see the final version of his fantasy. He died in 1985, three years before his wife completed the work with the help of architect Tom Oswalt.

The building, reminiscent of Barcelona's Parc Güell blended with American cake you'd think was topped with overmuch whipped cream, seems out of place even in such a heterogeneous neighborhood.

The white concrete flows from the decorative terminals to the roof tiles, *trencadis* (broken-tile mosaic or shardware) additions decorate the façade with its oval windows, and, down a side path, a statue adorns the back entrance.

Watts Towers, a sculpture consisting of 17 connected structures built between 1921 and 1954 by Italian immigrant construction worker Simon Rodia, is another tribute to Gaudí. The towers, in the poor neighborhood of Watts (southern LA, just above Compton) are victims of their own success and mentioned in all the guidebooks.

FREDERICK R. WEISMAN ART FOUNDATION

(21)

Maybe the world's finest private art collection

Frederick R. Weisman Art Foundation
Holmby Hills (exact address given at time of booking, by phone or email)
+1 (310) 277-5321
tours@weismanfoundation.org
weismanfoundation.org/home
Free guided tours Monday to Friday, 10:30am and 2pm, by appointment only

Magritte, Picasso, Warhol, Rauschenberg, Rothko, Haring, Cézanne, Giacometti, Noguchi, Calder, Kandinsky, Miró ... Hidden in the heart of an extraordinary villa nestled in the hills is simply one of America's most important post-war art collections. To top it all for chic, few know of its existence.

Frederick Weisman, born in Minnesota, was an entrepreneur who had huge success in commercial distribution (in the 1970s, he developed the company Mid-Atlantic Toyota, the first to import the renowned brand of Japanese cars to the Unites States).

Weisman, together with his two wives (Marcia Simon and, later, Billie Milam, one-time curator of local institutions LACMA and Getty) amassed a vertiginous and extremely coherent collection of contemporary art over the years. In 1982, Weisman purchased this Mediterranean Revival-style villa in order to share his finest discoveries. His plan was to make it a house where visitors would be welcome to stroll around, rather than an austere museum.

The result is spectacular, in that the walls, wood-inlaid floors and hand-painted ceilings showcase an incredible variety of paintings and sculptures of incredible quality and major artistic importance. The greatest names of the 20th century are gathered here, as if enveloped in its beauty.

The house and garden, as well as an annex on the Pepperdine University campus in Malibu, are accessible to the public by reservation.

Part of the collection is in the Frederick R. Weisman Art Museum in Minneapolis, a quirky building on the University of Minnesota campus. The structure was designed in 1993 by Frank Gehry as a tribute to the local boy (who died a year later). It resembles an angular version of the architect's LA masterpiece, the Walt Disney Concert Hall, thus closing the circle. Over 25,000 works from private and public collections share the spotlight.

MONTHLY OPEN DAY AT GREYSTONE MANSION

(22)

Notorious scene of an unsolved crime

905 Loma Vista Drive
+1 (310) 286-0119
greystonemansion.org
Grounds open 10am–5pm in winter, 6pm in summer
Closed Thanksgiving, Christmas Day and for filming
Mansion open to the public once a month by reservation
Annual mystery evenings: The Manor

Spiderman, *Columbo*, *Alias*, *Austin Powers*, *The Social Network*, *The Muppets*, *Air Force One*, *Mission: Impossible*, *X-Men* (the famous gardens of Professor Xavier's School for Gifted Youngsters), not to mention countless clips and TV shows: Greystone Mansion, as well as

the surrounding park, is unquestionably the "natural" location most used by Hollywood. And yet, though many couch potato film buffs would recognize the site at a glance, few locals make the effort to explore it, and very few know its history.

While the mansion is open to visitors only for special events (music, theatre, etc.), or once a month with a ranger, the park is public, free and open year-round. Visitors can sample Beverly Hills luxury without the stars and their paparazzi, surrounded by the splendor of magnificent English gardens.

Stretching out below is a superb view of Beverly Flats and West Hollywood, with the downtown skyline in the distance.

A mysterious assassination, restaged once a year

The mansion was the scene of a true-life drama when, in 1929, five months after moving in, estate owner Edward "Ned" Doheny was murdered there by his assistant, Hugh Plunket, who was found dead by his side.

Ned's widow, Lucy Smith, remarried and continued to live in the 55-room, neoclassical Gothic-style mansion while police and journalists were still investigating the mysterious murder, which was never solved.

Each year in January, you can take part in a costume "re-enactment" of the crime scene, during a Clue-style evening billed as The Manor.

As always in Hollywood, other versions recount either a suicide of the heir after dark stories of bribes involving his oil-tycoon father or a story of forbidden love that ended badly.

The mansion that inspired a novel that was later filmed there ...

Ned Doheny's father, Edward L. Doheny, inspired Upton Sinclair's 1927 novel *Oil!*, which Paul Thomas Anderson freely adapted for the cinema in 2007 with *There Will Be Blood*. Some of the scenes were shot at Greystone Mansion, such as the iconic final clash in the bowling alley – the stately home's basement.

PLAQUE MARKING THE EXACT CENTER OF THE CITY

㉓

Unearthing this treasure is a quite an achievement

Franklin Canyon Park

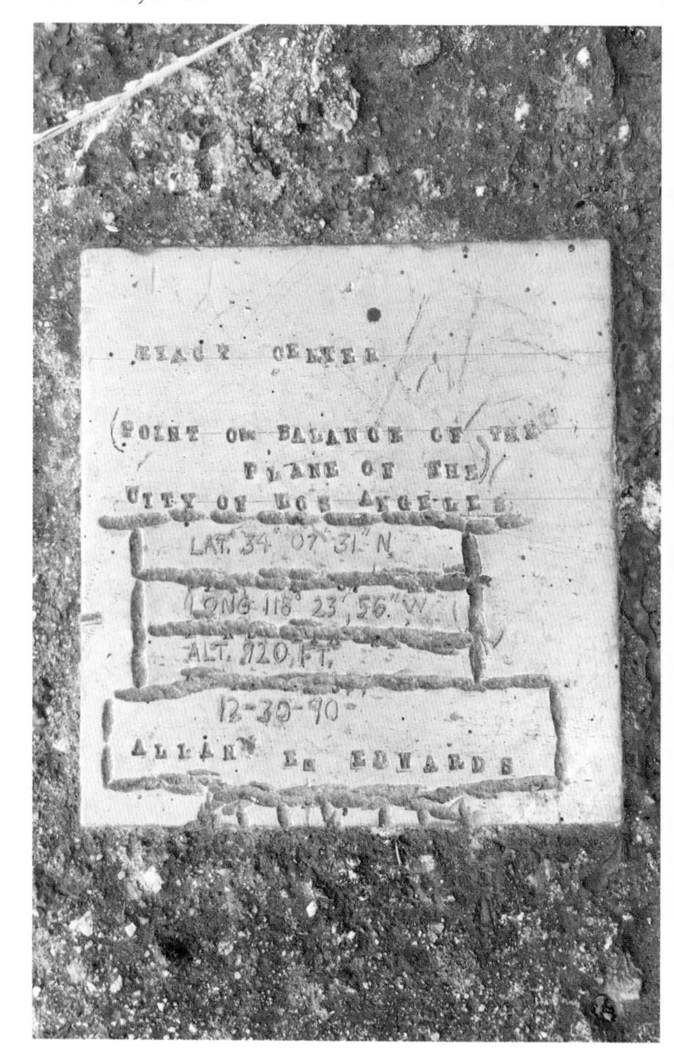

In her 1937 autobiography, feminist writer and art collector Gertrude Stein is said to have written of her childhood town, Oakland, "there is no there there." A phrase since taken up in everyday American parlance, to emphasize the absence of a significant characteristic of a place or situation. Kind of like "move along, there's nothing to see." This aphorism is unfortunately very often applied to this corner of California. LA is constantly criticized by certain tourists for its lack of interest and "center." Indeed, where is central LA? Is it Downtown? Hollywood? Santa Monica? Griffith Park? Mid-City? LAX? Where is LA's authentic center of gravity hidden?

In an attempt to answer this haunting question, Allan Edwards, geologist and tourist guide by trade, fixed a homemade metal plate to the ground in the middle of the little-known Franklin Canyon Park in 1990. Though it was never recognized by the National Park Service, it has become the unofficial topographical center of the city.

Finding it will take patience and fortitude. Leave your car in the main lot of the park (a dusty and unpaved area, to be precise), walk to the second section of the lot, higher up. From there, take the Chaparral Trail, a very steep path on which you'll need to fork right after a few yards. A narrow ditch, with a large bush to the left, marks the start of another parallel path, where a charming wooden bridge awaits. Then you'll see the main walkway in the middle.

There, a mini mound of earth supports the plaque, which very few locals or tourists have ever heard of. Congratulations! You're part of the even more select club of the rare few who've actually seen it. These words are engraved on it: *Exact Center. Point of balance of the plane of the city of Los Angeles*, followed by GPS coordinates and the date, December 30, 1990, then the signature of Allan E. Edwards. This might not do much for you, unless it's the immense satisfaction of having unearthed the center of a town without a center, in the middle of nowhere: finally, there is indeed a "there there."

HIKE ON THE LA-96C ANTI-MISSILE DEFENSE SITE

24

Trekking in the traces of the Cold War

San Vicente Mountain Park
17500 Mulholland Drive, Encino
+1 (310) 858-7272
lamountains.com
Open and accessible year-round

When you're exploring San Vicente Mountain Park between Bel-Air and Encino, in the mountains above Santa Monica, the first few miles of this loop (total almost 9 miles/14 km) give little away.

Only on arrival at the summit, at the edge of this unpaved section of Mulholland Drive, do the strange remains catch your eye: their radar platform, antennae, and watchtower are straight out of a military propaganda film.

And for good reason: the 360° view is from a genuine missile-control site, where interpretive panels reveal the martial truth: from 1956 to 1968, at the height of the Cold War, Los Angeles was surrounded by 16 anti-aircraft bases. Radar and computer systems known as Nike-Ajax (after the Greek goddess of victory and the celebrated Greek hero), aimed to repel any Russian planes by guiding supersonic missiles from the base at Sepulveda Basin in the event of nuclear attack, for immediate interception. Of course, no missiles ever would be fired, and most of today's citizens are unaware that they were once within a protective circle of military bases.

Yet, at the time, the threatened apocalypse was all over the newspapers and the TV news. The fear of nuclear attack from west or north stifled the spirit, videos prompted people to take shelter when the siren sounded, and successive groups manned these city observation bases on the orders of the Pentagon.

By the late 1960s, the Nike surveillance program was rendered obsolete by the development of ballistic missiles, new vehicles stealthier than a still-pervasive nuclear threat. The LA-96C base, along with the other 15, was offered to the State of California to be turned into regional parks, spurred by conservation agencies that had struggled to open these sites to the public, despite US government reluctance. But not all the observation bases have suffered the same fate: Malibu, for example, has been converted to a training camp for local firefighters, and Fort MacArthur is now a museum.

Note that you can drive to these impressive Cold War relics and park directly on the site, about a half mile (1 km) west of the unpaved section of Mulholland Drive, to enjoy its history while avoiding a pretty difficult hike.

SACRED WATER SOURCE OF THE TONGVA

(25)

On the lands of indigenous peoples

Serra Springs
11800 Texas Avenue
+1 (916) 445-7000
ohp.parks.ca.gov/ListedResources/Detail/522
Always visible from from the high school stadium

Tongva village replica
Heritage Park, 12100 Mora Drive, Santa Fe Springs
+1 (562) 946-6476
santafesprings.org
May–October, 7am–8pm weekdays, 9am–8pm weekends
End of October to end of April, 7am–5pm weekdays, 9am–5pm weekends
Park closed on public holidays

Before the first Spanish settlers established Mission San Gabriel Arcángel, the fourth Spanish mission in California (inaugurated around 1771), the Tongva Native Americans had lived on these lands for over 2,500 years. Hounded out, they were soon coerced into converting to Catholicism and moved to the mission site, where they were renamed "Gabrieleños," despite repeated attempts at rebellion. Previously their villages had dotted the coast and the Los Angeles Basin, forming complex societies around the rivers and springs.

Two of these springs can be seen on the University High School campus, well hidden in a patch of undergrowth, between classrooms and the sports field where the students train. To see them (through fencing), leave your car in the school parking lot and walk along the stadium grass to the northeast corner. The two springs are behind lush greenery near an inconspicuous plaque carrying the number 522 (all protected historic sites are numbered in LA).

In the city of Santa Fe Springs, part of the recently renovated Heritage Park has a reconstruction of a traditional site of great importance to aboriginal American Indian culture.

A replica of an original Tongva homestead stands among the trees. As they weren't a nomadic people, there's no teepee here, but rather a hut and canoe made from willow and hard-stemmed bulrush (a kind of rush). While these obviously aren't the originals, they're on land trod by the Tongva ancestors before their expulsion. It's a moving site that gives a good idea of what the life of pre-Columbian populations in this part of the globe might have been like.

The "Indian museum" ... and the cowboys

The most interesting artifacts from this almost extinct culture can be found at the Southwest Museum of the American Indian (234 Museum Drive, Mount Washington district), a superb facility opened in 1914 by the anthropologist and journalist Charles Lummis, founder of the Southwest Society, a California branch of the Archaeological Institute of America.

To see the other side of the story – the winners of this bloody conquest of the West – head for the Autry Museum of the American West (Griffith Park, 4700 Western Heritage Way), where the cowboys take precedence over the Indians.

CLAY SCULPTURES AT THE BHAGAVAD-GITA MUSEUM

(26)

Secrets and mysteries of a controversial branch of Hinduism

3764 Watseka Avenue
+1 (310) 845-9333
bgmuseum.com
Daily (except Tuesday), 10am–5pm
Restaurant Monday to Saturday, 11am–3pm and 5pm–8:30pm
Metro: Expo Line, Palms stop

The Bhagavad-gita (Song by God), an episode from the Mahabharata, a Sanskrit epic retracing the evolution of Hindu mythology, is one of the founding texts of Hinduism. Considered one of the world's greatest poems, it blends historical, mythological, and philosophical narratives, and is still revered today by millions of people both in India and abroad.

In 1977, a museum housing 11 dioramas of episodes from this sacred scripture opened in Culver City, at the heart of a very active Hare Krishna community. Note that although in India this movement is considered just one of the branches of Hinduism, in the West it's very

often referred to as a sect.

Swami Prabhupada, leader at the time and founder of the International Society for Krishna Consciousness (aka Hare Krishnas) in New York, had returned several times to his homeland to learn the techniques used in ancient India, in order to introduce them in the U.S. The sculptures were built by local devotees. Bamboo, rice straw and husk, along with various clays, were used to make the realistic, hand-painted dolls, each with their own mannerisms and character. Some have been fitted with an electric motor that animates them individually. The dioramas are all set to music.

In a mysterious and almost disturbing artificial twilight, a 45-minute self-guided tour lets you wander among the dioramas, read their stories and learn about transcendentalism.

Two guided tours of 60 and 90 minutes, respectively, are also on offer: they provide a better understanding of the challenges and aspirations of this little-known community.

The last option includes lunch at Govinda's, the adjoining top-notch vegetarian buffet. For more materialistic visitors, the devotees also have a souvenir shop chock-full of jewelry, clothes, musical instruments, books, and even CDs dedicated to Indian culture and its diverse religions and philosophies. Bottom line: this is an astonishing and sometimes intimidating journey through the twists and turns of the Hindu faith.

MUSEUM OF JURASSIC TECHNOLOGY

27

Bizarre relics of mysterious provenance

9341 Venice Blvd
310-836-6131
mjt.org
Thursday 2pm–8pm; Friday–Sunday 12noon–6pm

It's difficult to describe, and that's kind of the point. Officially, the Museum of Jurassic Technology calls itself "an educational institution dedicated to the advancement of knowledge and the public appreciation of the Lower Jurassic" – though exactly what that has to do with any of the museum's meticulous curations is anybody's guess.

The fact is, empirical truths are pretty hard to come by in this dense cabinet of curiosities, where elaborate fictions are presented seamlessly beside fantastical realities – all with hushed, quasi-scientific reverence.

Founded in 1988 by artists and curators Diana and David Hildebrand Wilson, the Museum of Jurassic Technology hides behind an innocuous storefront in Culver City. Covering two stories, this temple to the bizarre houses hundreds of relics of mysterious provenance, each willfully blurring the line between fact and fiction. Dioramas depicting LA's apocalypse-ready mobile homes, a fruit pit delicately engraved with the Crucifixion, a tribute to the dogs of the Soviet Space Program and a collection of decaying dices that once belonged to magician Ricky Jay – they're all here but they are just the tip of this alchemical iceberg.

Come to be puzzled, and stay for a cup of tea in the serene rooftop aviary, one of the most special and secret-feeling spaces in the city.

© Sgerbic

BIG LEBOWSKI APARTMENT

(28)

The Dude has left his mark everywhere

608 Venezia Avenue, Venice
House can be seen from the street
Metro: Expo Line, Palms stop

The Coen Brothers cult film *The Big Lebowski* (1998) has its fervent followers who can't help quoting the best lines whenever they open their mouths.

Although the incredible tales of Jeff "The Dude" Lebowski, played by Jeff Bridges, lead him to different LA locations through the city's variegated social strata, his escapade begins in this little house. It's where two thugs, mistaking The Dude for a millionaire of the same name, urinate on his rug. In fact it's a block of six modest bungalows, which have been resold several times since the filming, the last time in 2012 for the tidy sum of $2.3 million.

Nowadays, The Dude, unemployed idler and bowling fanatic, would be hard-pressed to afford the rent in such a neighborhood – the epitome of on-trend LA.

Whereas the interiors were shot in recording studios in West Hollywood, the small street wedged in the gap between Venice Boulevard and Abbot Kinney is home to the white-painted pointed roofs of the "Big Lebowski set," as real estate agents have tagged it. This street is also used in the scenes where his rich namesake's limo drops Bridges at home, and when he discovers a detective trailing him.

Pilgrimage for Dude fans

Among the other *Big Lebowski* pilgrimage sites that obsessive moviegoers try to find, check out the splendid Sheats-Goldstein residence above Holmby Hills, a modernist architecture marvel with its embossed concrete roof.

Johnie's Coffee Shop, the most traditional of diners, closed in 2000 and is now used as a backdrop for other Hollywood productions.

And don't forget forget San Pedro's Sunken City (see page 222), where friends of Donny (Steve Buscemi) fail in their attempts to scatter his ashes.

Finally, the film also features the wood-paneled living room, grand staircase and corridors of Greystone Mansion (see page 106), a key location. They're all among the many cultural markers that make LA a unique playground for cinephile treasure hunters, and not only for Coen Brothers fans.

THE MOSAIC TILE HOUSE

(29)

A crazy house completely covered with trencadis *(broken-tile mosaic)*

1116 Palms, Venice
cheripann.com/The_Mosaic_Tile_House.html
Saturday 1pm–4pm, reservation recommended at mosaictilehouse@mac.com
Free for children under 12

With infectious humor, Gonzalo Duran, an artist living in this incredible Venice house, for a few hours once a week delights in taking a tour of the property, stressing that he and his partner, Cheri Pann, actually live here all year round. However, once in the garden, the human and material cohabitation frankly doesn't seem ideal: everywhere

shards of glass, porcelain, ceramic, and metal (for the few doors that exist) entangle and hang from the trees, barely letting visitors past. Visitors are forced into contortions to access the patio, not touching anything so as not to damage the kitchen, which seems so fragile, or the delicately-placed paintings.

The material of these unique mosaics is sometimes very crude, like the mug handles or entire statuettes stuck here and there, making the house, workshop, and passageways look like a constantly moving snake ready to devour you.

The backyard is more airy, featuring portraits painted by Cheri and Gonzalo's burlesque machinations. He continues the tour with a stream of jokes, before the ritual of selfies in the alleyway; it's original, its walls covered with shards of glass refracting its own image.

Cheri, an American from the Boyle Heights neighborhood, has made color her life's work, painting and printing nonstop. The development of this endless array of mosaics began in 1994, after they bought the house, which had a garden big enough to accommodate an artist's studio. Since then, art has taken over everything. "We started with the bathroom, where we wanted to install some little tiles, and since then we've never looked back," says 74-year-old Gonzalo, born in Mexico and raised in East LA. The couple hope that their unique home will one day be listed on the National Register of Historic Places by the Los Angeles Cultural Heritage Commission.

Meantime, the Gaudí-style *trencadis* (broken-tile mosaic) continues to dazzle, an art form favored by renowned artists who don't seem to have lost their way at all, nor are they finding it all too much. "There's a balance in all this, we find ourselves here," Gonzalo concludes mischievously.

Phantasma Gloria

Known as *Phantasma Gloria*, an incredible 22-foot-tall sculpture made from bottles and glass objects can be seen from the street in the garden of a house in the Echo Park district.
This is the ever-evolving work of artist Randlett (Randy) Lawrence, who'll be delighted to show you around his colorful Eden, as long as you've booked in advance.
A real gem.
1648 Lemoyne Street, Los Angeles
+1 (213) 278-1508
Weekend tours from 10am to 4pm

VENICE BEACH RAINBOW LIFEGUARD STATION

30

A moving tribute to one of LA's most iconic beaches

Venice Pride Flag Lifeguard Tower
998 Ocean Front Walk, in Venice (end of Brooks Avenue)
(424) 330-7788
venicepride.org
Daily 7am–8pm
Metro: Expo Line, Downtown Santa Monica stop

You don't have to be part of the LGBTQIA+ community to appreciate the unique colors of the rescue tower at the end of Brooks Avenue. With its rainbow robes, this *Baywatch*-style shelter, which protects the best-known lifeguards on the planet, is certainly the most Instagrammable along the entire California coast. And its tribute-like story is especially moving.

Flashback: for many years the west of the city was a peaceful haven for those "on the fringes" of good society. But after West Hollywood became the nation's first "gay city" in 1984, there was a slow exodus to the east. The phenomenon was so vast that the last gay bar on the West Side closed in 2016.

In hopes of reviving the community west of Highway 405, which separates two very different views of life in LA, the Venice Pride Organization envisioned a series of events that same year. Artists Patrick Marston and Michael Brunt were commissioned to repaint one of the iconic rescue towers, traditionally sky blue, during Pride Month. Note that this stretch of beach had just been renamed Bill Rosendahl Memorial Beach.

Bill Rosendahl was a member of the city council from 2005 to 2013. Openly gay, he was the driving force behind the Expo Line, which now connects the city center to the beach. University professor and TV anchor in another life, before devoting himself to public affairs, he died in 2016. The tower, which was supposed to wear its new clothes only temporarily, was then saved from a humdrum life by militant actor Colin Campbell, who circulated a petition to preserve the shimmering colors.

The installation is now permanent, so, whatever your leanings, grab your best swim gear to come and celebrate diversity at Venice Beach. And don't forget your camera. You could kill two birds with one stone by capturing in a single frame the rainbow adorning the tower and the famous red buoys, straight out of one of the state's most iconic TV series.

THE "OFFICIAL" TERMINUS OF ROUTE 66

(31)

Several possible traces of the route

The "official" terminus of Route 66
Intersection of Lincoln and Olympic boulevards in Santa Monica
Other locations between Santa Monica and Needles, last city before the Arizona state line

Unlike the other states it runs through, Route 66, however mythical, isn't easy to follow in California, especially from Santa Monica Pier, even though a camera-friendly sign marks the route's end (or beginning, depending on which direction you were heading).

This is due to "alignments" made over the years, especially when highways were built around and through the heart of LA, which have multiplied the possible traces from downtown to Pasadena. At first, the terminus wasn't at the famous pier, but at the intersection of Lincoln and Olympic boulevards, far from the beach, before an artificial junction

leading to the ocean was built.

Located at this original corner, the vintage Googie-style Penguin coffee shop, revered by buffs and bikers and later converted to a dentist's office in 1991, has now been taken over by a fast-food chain that plans to install a prominent sign indicating the "true" end of the route, as it was in 1936.

Further east, at Highland Park, successive alignments have created three possible routes: a 1932 realignment, a section along Figueroa Avenue (1936–1940), and a section leading to the Arroyo Seco Parkway (1940–1964) before the latter became the first highway to follow Route 66.

They may not be the most spectacular, but the first few miles to Needles, the last city before the Arizona state line, turn up some interesting sights. From the mansions and neon signs of Pasadena, the teepee-shaped Wigwam Motel, the first US McDonald's (later converted to a museum in honor of the two fast-food founders, brothers Richard and Maurice McDonald) in San Bernardino, to the orange-shaped kiosks at Fontana, they all have indelible traces of Route 66 in their DNA.

GRUNION RUN

When the beach sparkles in the moonlight

At many Los Angeles County beaches and throughout Southern California, late March to early June
Find program and best spots at californiabeaches.com

Between the end of March and the beginning of June, smack in the middle of the night, Santa Monica beach regularly comes alive with clusters of people bundled up, wearing headlamps and carrying buckets. Whole families gather to try to catch a fish that is only found here – the grunion.

"Grunion (Leuresthes tenuis) are bony fish from the Atherinopsidae family," according to Wikipedia. Native to the Pacific coast, on a strip stretching from Monterey Bay to Baja California (Mexico), they look like small sardines or glass eels.

But beyond their endemic nature, it's their fascinating mode of reproduction, exclusively at night, that offers fish enthusiasts and curious visitors an annual unique (and organized) event: for a few weeks, hundreds of thousands of female fish voluntarily beach themselves to spawn, before the males fertilize the eggs – also out of the water. The result is spectacular: some of the beaches start to sparkle with the countless tiny fish fluttering in the moonlight.

In her tale *Grayson* (2007), Lynne Cox, a well-known professional open-water swimmer turned writer, describes the process in great detail: "Once a female reaches the beach, she digs a hole in the sand with her tail, then wiggles back and forth, drilling herself down into the soft wet sand until she is buried all the way up to her lips. There she lays up to three thousand eggs at once and one of the male grunion arches around her and releases his milt to fertilize the eggs. Then the adult grunion swim back to sea while the eggs incubate in the warm sand for ten days ... It was a great attraction in Southern California. In summer, I would meet friends on the beach on moonlit nights and wait for the grunion. We'd spread out our large bright-striped beach blankets ... beyond the reach of the incoming waves."

She also explains that you can have fun catching the fish and releasing them right away. There's no need to eat them after enjoying the show. A California fishing license is actually required for participants over the age of 16, who should bag only a "reasonable" number to avoid waste and maybe upset the environmental balance.

Finally, in order to pay this miracle of nature all due respect, digging a hole in the sand to trap the grunion is also banned, or you face a fine. And it's strongly recommended to keep as quiet as possible and not use too bright a flashlight.

FRANK GEHRY RESIDENCE

(33)

Private residence of a master of his art

Frank Gehry residence
1002 22nd Street, Santa Monica
foga.com
View from the street year-round

When you arrive at the corner of 22nd Street and Washington Avenue in Santa Monica, it's hard to determine what style of architecture this typical suburban house represents, with its metal sheeting and wood-framed asymmetrical windows. Yet one thing is certain – the name Frank Gehry instantly springs to mind as his trademark style is so clearly recognizable. The most celebrated North American architect of his generation once lived here, and rightfully so as it was this "renovation" that boosted his career in the late 1970s.

Protrusions of aluminum and low-cost chain-link fencing jostle for space, coupled with huge sloping glass windows that reveal the original, rather modest frame of the two-story house. The quirky structure is reminiscent of both the Walt Disney Concert Hall in downtown LA with its corrugated panels – a showcase for the Los Angeles Philharmonic – and the Fondation Louis Vuitton in Paris with its chrysalis-like glass roof, two of Gehry's most iconic achievements.

To some extent, the earthy tones of his residence are a response to the building Gehry designed for the Chiat/Day advertising agency in 1991, before his major projects for the city. At 340 Main Street, Venice Beach, this easy-to-identify structure, now Google offices, has a striking street-facing façade centerpiece: a three-story sculpture known as *Giant Binoculars*, by Claes Oldenburg and Coojse van Bruggen.

The 1920s bungalow that Gehry called home lacks the majesty of his later achievements, but it illustrates the tenets of the deconstructivist movement quite clearly. Of course, like any daring architectural experiment, it was loathed for a long time before finally being accepted, especially by neighbors who delighted in emptying their garbage cans into the garden. How disappointed they must have been when they saw, over the years, that the distinguished resident had changed the face of the city forever. Multiple projects in this corner of southern California have raised his prestige exponentially.

After years of saying he wanted to "liberate himself and family from the influence of this eccentric residence," Gehry collaborated with his son, architect Sam Gehry, to design a new, more traditional yet markedly post-modern residence in Santa Monica, where the architect now lives.

EAMES HOUSE

Like a Mondrian origami

Eames House
Case Study House No. 8
203 North Chautauqua Boulevard, Pacific Palisades
eamesfoundation.org/house/eames-house
+1 (310) 459-9663
Reservation required (at least 48 hours in advance)
Exteriors: $10, free for students; Indoors: $250 for one to two people

Ray and Charles Eames were undoubtedly the most important designer couple of the 20th century. Their iconic furniture (notably the Eames Lounge Chair, 6 million of which have been sold worldwide since its creation in 1956) has brought together cutting-edge design and mass production.

This modernist building of concrete, black steel and glass, clad in Mondrian-like panels in primary colors, was designed by the Eames' for the Case Study House Program, an essentially Californian architectural experience led between 1945 and 1966, the aim of which was to build economic and functional individual homes. "The house must be capable of duplication and in no sense be an individual 'performance'," the program announced at the time, giving rise to 36 atypical projects that blended the simplest of designs with the noblest of aspirations.

In 1949, this Case Study House No. 8, located in the Pacific Palisades neighborhood of LA, became the personal home and studio of the Eames couple, who modified it to suit their needs, creating their perfect design space. Following the rhythm of its inhabitants, so demanding in their search for simplicity, this home-studio evolved constantly. The couple lived here until their deaths in 1978 and 1988, respectively.

The house is now a museum, but one that plays hard to get. The rules are strict: no on-site parking (ideally get dropped off), reservation required (at least 48 hours in advance, but a week ahead is recommended), photos are prohibited inside the house, and the visit is quite pricey.

But this is truly a unique experience. Nature is omnipresent as the leaves of the trees play against the glass walls and birdsong fills the space. The scent of raw materials pervades the air and everything has an "unfinished" air about it, yet it is a house that feels lived in. Far from home, you'll feel at home here, in this museum open to the four winds.

HIKING AT MURPHY RANCH

Abandoned Nazi camp

Sullivan Fire Road, Pacific Palisades
Accessible year-round
Free
Via Casale Road, north of Pacific Palisades, Interstate 405 or Highway 1 (CA-1 N)

Hiking is a cult in Los Angeles. This isn't strictly speaking a mountain hike in the usual sense, with bivouac and sixty-pound backpacks, but rather a sporty morning or afternoon walk on the city hills to relax, and sometimes to see and be seen – movie stars sharing ordinary folks' interests.

In contrast to the concrete tracery of the interchanges and structures – the most commonly accepted cliché evoking the "capital" of Southern California – is a range of hills, summits, and canyons where you can escape the ebb and flow of the city in just a quarter of an hour, tops. And there are plenty of surprises in store once you're entrenched in the dirt roads.

It's not rare to come across coyotes or mountain lions (pumas) watching visitors from a distance, amid the typical flora of semi-arid climates. Not a sound to be heard, change of scenery guaranteed.

But Murphy Ranch is among the best at this pursuit. Imagine: a path steep enough to test your stamina, 500 artificial steps plunging into the depths of a canyon, and, suddenly coming into view, old structures that were once habitable, now covered with greenery and graffiti. And a backstory ... what a story!

This story goes back to the 1930s, long before Charles Manson and his "family" terrorized the region. Before World War II, a mysterious German named Herr Schmidt is said to have incited a wealthy local couple, Winona and Norman Stephens, to build an ideal and self-sufficient city to prepare for the coming of global Nazi rule, which was supposed to extend to the United States after German troops had won the war. The idea was to build a hidden base to support the cause and take refuge in the event that the American government fell. When the US entered the war in 1941, work stopped on the building site, the remains of which are now uncovered. The four-story mansion, a reflection of the splendor of Nazi high society, was never built, and 50 arrests were made at the ranch just after the attack on Pearl Harbor.

This popular playground for local graffiti artists is regularly fenced off by City Hall, which also barricades the entrances to the buildings. The 4-mile (6.5 km) round trip hike is an exploration of the vicissitudes of time, almost in urbex (urban exploration) mode, as new ramblers routinely reopen the condemned route.

At Topanga Canyon, once past the fence, the first dank track and the steps, you'll discover the walls of the barn and a power plant, like makeshift bunkers, now discolored and distorted after years of abandonment. The same is true of the concrete slabs where there used to be gardens. The remains of a hangar and a water tank complete the picture. The cool air permeates here earlier than down in the valley, charging the atmosphere with menace and inviting the ghosts of a frightening alternate history on a haunted hike.

ABANDONED SETS FROM M*A*S*H

36

In Malibu, relics of a fictional Korean war

Malibu Creek State Park
1925 Las Virgenes Road (then follow Crags Road)
+1 (818) 880-0367
malibucreekstatepark.org/MASH.html
Park open sunrise through sunset

Breathtaking views, rugged peaks, trekking through the sycamores, climbing, a volcanic stone natural pool, a dam, rolling hills covered with grasses and chaparral scrub, and streams – located north of the city that gives it its name, Malibu Creek State Park in the Santa Monica Mountains, once the home of Chumash Native Americans, is an exceptional location covering 20 square miles.

M*A*S*H (Mobile Army Surgical Hospital), the iconic and multiple award-winning American TV series, was filmed here from 1972 to 1983.

The 20th Century Fox studios owned a ranch used as the set for filming this satirical take on the daily life of a surgical field unit, supposedly in Korea during the war. The 251 episodes of the series haven't only left their mark on our memories.

A number of props, from vehicles to information boards to tables, were left behind when the studio donated the ranch to the city and it became part of the park.

Local hikers, keen to preserve this wonderful trail, began to promote the relics. Eaten away by rust and almost unrecognizable, they were restored in the 2000s, until the Woolsey Fire of November 2018 again damaged part of the site.

But it's still accessible by following Crags Road, the main trail and a 5-mile hike with a slight elevation of about 200 feet. Parking is at 1925 Las Virgenes Road.

The relics of the M*A*S*H sets can be seen about halfway along. Alternate routes exist, such as the South Grassland Trail and the Cistern Trail.

© Marty B

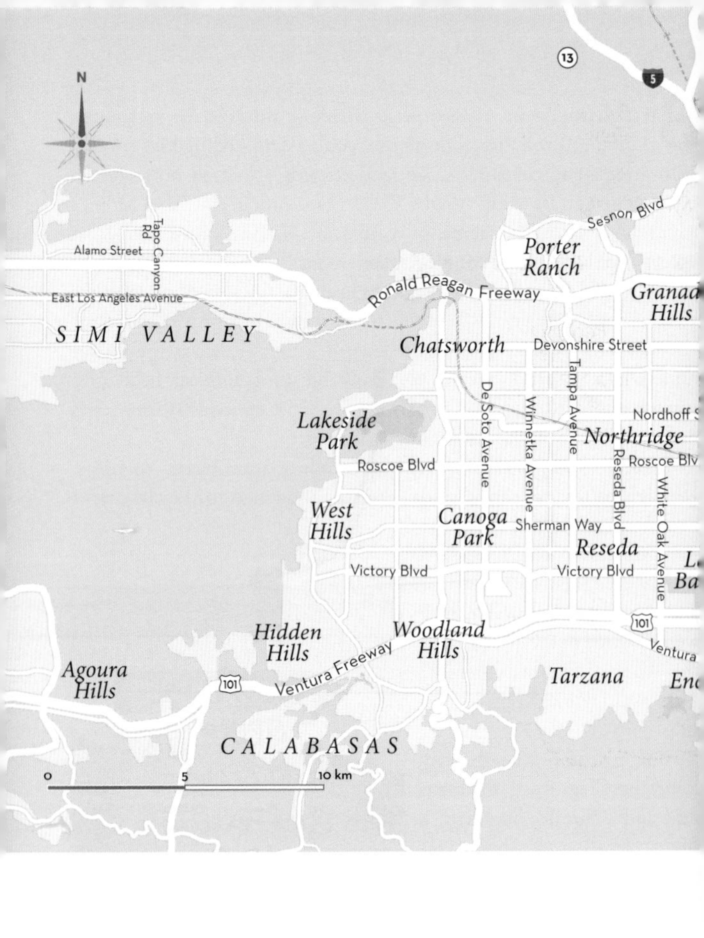

San Fernando Valley

1. BAXTER STREET — 138
2. MUSEUM OF THE HOLY LAND — 140
3. WALK ALONGSIDE THE LOS ANGELES RIVER — 142
4. GRAVES OF CAROLE LOMBARD AND CLARK GABLE — 144
5. NEON MUSEUM — 146
6. RUNWAY OF DISUSED GRAND CENTRAL AIR TERMINAL — 148
7. SOUTH KEYSTONE STREET — 150

(8) WALT'S BARN 152

(9) ALFRED HITCHCOCK'S BUNGALOW 5195 154

(10) THE ORIGINAL ROUTE OF THE FIRST CAMPO DE CAHUENGA MISSION 156

(11) "FREEDOM BOULEVARD" BUILDING BY THIERRY NOIR 158

(12) DONALD C. TILLMAN WATER RECLAMATION PLANT 160

(13) DOOR TO ROOM A113 OF CALARTS 162

BAXTER STREET

1

One of the steepest streets in the States

Always accessible

San Francisco, originally built on seven hills, has the reputation of being the city with the most precipitous streets. But a close runner-up is Los Angeles, despite its image of wide, flat and monotonous highways barely disturbed by neon lights and palm trees. The

unrelenting canyons that make up LA's less accessible spaces have some amazing hidden passageways, like at Highland Park, San Pedro or here in Silverlake, near the reservoir.

With its 32% slope (equivalent to about 18 degrees), Baxter Street, just off Highway 2, is one of the steepest streets in the nation and a notorious accident site when rare showers drench the city. In 2018, fed up with skidding cars careening into their gardens or up against their fences, folks were writing to the authorities and to GPS and mobile app developers to demand improved traffic flow in the form of algorithms to avoid their street at all costs. Since a fire truck also has been stuck on the ridge, discussions are ongoing to find a viable solution and alternate routes.

The 10 steepest streets in the USA

Even crazier, Eldred Street (near Mount Washington) and 28th Street (San Pedro) have a 33% and 33.3% slope, respectively, but they are not as long and busy as their big Silverlake sibling.

This trio of impressive statistics makes the state of California the holder of seven of the 10 steepest streets (a fourth, Fargo Street, is in Los Angeles, two are in San Francisco and the last is in Spring Valley).

And just to show off at Trivial Pursuit: the other three are in Honokaa (Hawaii) and Pittsburgh (Pennsylvania).

And that makes ten!

LA's shortest and longest streets

Powers Place, a 13-foot strip in the Pico-Union district connecting Alvarado Terrace and South Bonnie Braie Street, was named after Pomeroy Wills Powers, a lawyer from Kansas City who became a LA City Council president. LA's shortest street, it barely leaves a car enough room to make a tight U-turn.

The longest street in LA is the unmissable Sepulveda Boulevard: this mastodon, sections of which are known as Highway 1 (the iconic Pacific coastal route), stretches 42.8 miles from Long Beach to San Fernando.

MUSEUM OF THE HOLY LAND

②

By the explorer thought to have inspired Indiana Jones

Holyland Exhibition
2215 Lake View Avenue
(323) 664-3162
Daily 7am–7pm
Guided tour lasting two hours, reservation only – call first

"Hollywood waits for people to die, and then it takes ownership of their stories without having to pay anything to rights holders."

It is with a touch of mischief and disillusionment that Betty Shepard, an unusual guide, begins her tour of LA's most unlikely museum.

Secretive, hidden, and one could even say private given the lack of visitors some days, this museum has nevertheless been the setting for priceless treasures since 1924. And the most fascinating thing about it is the persistent rumor that its founder, Antonia F. Futterer, inspired George Lucas to create the character of Dr. Henry Walton Jones, Jr., better known as Indiana Jones, archeologist by trade.

Futterer was an autodidact, or self-taught person. Having narrowly escaped death at the age of 24 (saved, the story goes, by his belief in the Bible), he became a mystic and set out to find the Ark of the Covenant, the legendary gold-plated wooden chest said to contain the Ten Commandments revealed to Moses on Mount Sinai. To this end he settled in Palestine, then Jerusalem, all the while amassing a collection of Syrian, Ethiopian, Egyptian, Israeli, and Palestinian artifacts. Now, he'd be described as a tomb raider, but in those days, he enjoyed a certain freedom to accomplish his life's work. And although Futterer, unlike Indiana Jones, never found the Ark (which some locate in the Aksum region of Ethiopia), the rest of his treasure is housed in five rooms filled floor-to-ceiling with collectibles you sometimes can't make head nor tail of, other than as multiple interpretations of scriptures, mainly of the monotheistic religions.

The room devoted to Syria is filled with marquetry furniture of incredible finesse, made in Damascus. A game table that graces the center of the room, encrusted with inland pearls, is alone worth the trip. Another room gives star billing to the secrets of the pharaohs (including a sarcophagus thousands of years old), and a third to archeology, with some objects of dubious origin.

The timeless souvenir shop, upstairs, is a replica of souks from Jerusalem to Beirut, complete with carpets, jewelry, and lamps. The auditorium on the ground floor contains an interesting simplified graphic presentation of an authentic 18th-century edition of the Bible, as well as a world map attempting (clumsily) to trace the different branches of human ancestry. Dressed in Bedouin gear, our guide gracefully passes from room to room and, surprisingly, doesn't take it all too seriously, despite the solemnity of the place. "I don't think Jesus would approve of any of the monotheistic religions if He came back to Earth today," she finishes with a smile.

WALK ALONGSIDE THE LOS ANGELES RIVER

③

River rehab

Los Angeles County, 51 miles from Calabasas to Long Beach
lariver.org (general information)
Wednesday–Sunday, 10am–4pm
Canoes and kayaks: +1 (323) 392-4247
lariverexpeditions.org
Paddles: lariverkayaks.com

A river in Los Angeles? For non-locals, the river's existence was long considered incongruous, although it runs for nearly 51 miles from Calabasas to Long Beach, skirting Griffith Park. And for good reason: the Los Angeles River had been neglected for a long time, becoming a rarely frequented no man's land sometimes used as a movie set, notably for Ryan Gosling's speeding car in *Drive* (2011).

But in recent years the river has been brought back into fashion by a number of restoration programs that led to the opening of a first section of cycle path in 1997. Nowadays, bikes can take two segments. One is a trail that runs from the Walt Disney studios alongside Highway 5 to Elysian Park and is dotted with cafes, such as the Spoke Bicycle Cafe in Frogtown, where cyclists can have their bikes fixed while enjoying a sandwich. The second segment, 20 miles long, runs from Commerce to Long Beach.

For those not so keen on two wheels, there are other options for exploring the river: pedestrian and equestrian trails of different lengths where you can see a variety of bird life (duck, great blue heron, cormorant, etc.), fishing spots, as well as kayaking and canoeing. Two sections of the meandering, comma-shaped waters, declared "navigable" in 2010, are open to water sports (Elysian Valley and San Fernando Valley), from Memorial Day (end of May) to September 30.

This wide range of activities has helped restore the image of this once-luxuriant heritage, which had devastated part of the urban development in its path. The river overflowed in the heavy rains of February 1938, flooding the area. That marked the end of the natural river. To protect local residents, the city opted to pour concrete over the riverbed and surround it with fencing, converting it into a "highway".

It's a term that unfortunately became quite fitting with the state's long periods of drought, when the river regularly ran dry. Paying tribute through recreational use is the least we can do to give it a new lease on life.

GRAVES OF CAROLE LOMBARD AND CLARK GABLE ④

Whiff of scandal at the cemetery

Forest Lawn Memorial Park Cemetery
1712 South Glendale Avenue, Glendale
+1 (888) 204-3131 (from United States) or +1 (323) 254-3131 (international)
forestlawn.com/parks/glendale
Daily 8am–6pm

Like all Hollywood scripts, including those that matchmake movie stars off-screen, this story is full of difficult-to-decipher mysteries and things left unsaid.

Carole Lombard and Clark Gable, two of the most adored and acclaimed stars of 1930s cinema, married in 1939 and are buried side by side: so far, so good.

But when the names of their past lovers also feature a few steps away, in the same crypt of the same cemetery, things get more interesting. So now you have the perfect excuse to visit the magnificent Forest Lawn Cemetery at Glendale, where a host of other celebrities are buried.

A stroll around the bucolic landscape is alone worth the trip, but at the same time it's a chance to pay your last respects to assorted showbiz figures (Michael Jackson lies here, for example). Forest Lawn is an institution.

In 1942, when Lombard, the leading actress of her generation, died

tragically, Gable was inconsolable. The unforgettable Rhett Butler of *Gone with the Wind* was barely able to finish the film he was making at the time, the romantic war drama *Somewhere I'll Find You*. He lost over 40 lbs, drowned his sorrows in alcohol for a time, then enlisted in the US military, or so the official version goes. When he died in 1960 he was buried next to the woman he'd always called the "love of his life." And Lombard's tomb does bear the inscription "Carole Lombard Gable."

Except, after Lombard's death, Gable remarried twice. His last union, with Kathleen "Kay" Williams, produced his only biological son – born four months after the actor's death. Yet he had always refused to provide for the upbringing of Judy Lewis (born 1935), the daughter he had with actress Loretta Young. Kay Williams, who took Gable's name at their wedding, is buried a few plots along.

Carole Lombard fans, for their part, maintain that Gable's fickle nature, and especially his supposed liaison with Lana Turner during the infamous filming of *Somewhere I'll Find You*, is the reason why Lombard wanted to cut short a tour in support of Allied troops and fly home. Her plane crashed after a supply stop in Las Vegas on January 16, 1942. That very morning she had refused to let her mother, who was killed in the same accident and is buried nearby, take the train. This is all the more curious as, according to the actress herself, her only true love was a certain Russ Columbo, a young singer she met when they were only 25, who died suddenly a year later, in 1934. And where is this Russ buried? A few yards away, in the crypt opposite. Convenient.

NEON MUSEUM

5

Gaudy art back in fashion

Museum of Neon Art (MONA)
216 South Brand Boulevard, Glendale
+1 (818) 696-2149
neonmona.org
Thursday–Saturday 12 noon–7pm, Sunday 12 noon–5pm
Neon Cruise: a few dates a year, book online

It's hard to find a more iconic craft than neon lighting in LA, where, from the 1920s onwards, the façades and roofs of buildings bloomed with eye-catching commercial signs, with the aim of luring drivers down the avenues where the car rules.

Disgraced by the close connections their imagery had with film noir, crime, risky motels and shady bars, followed by the loss of interest in the flashy esthetic of the time in the late '80s, neon signs have been making a triumphant comeback since the start of the new millennium. They are now viewed as a form of rehabilitated art (cool once again, with modern pieces in production), historic artifacts and the statement of a glorious and creative past.

After 34 years downtown, the Museum of Neon Art reopened in 2016 in Glendale, in a brand new space that, although not big enough to hold the entire collection, has the merit of welcoming regularly changing exhibits.

The electric and kinetic arts are also on show in a festival of flashing or static lights. On the borderline between physics and chemistry, the art of neon in all its forms is tastefully highlighted, from the Brown Derby restaurant's famous hat to plasma clocks, via themes renewed every three months (women, cars ...).

Finding the museum couldn't be easier: a huge figure rescued from the demolition of the Virginia Court Motel (Meridian, Mississippi) swims across the roof. There's also a replica of the swimmer diving in West Hollywood (easy to spot her when driving along Santa Monica Boulevard).

Learn how to make your own neon

MONA has had an idea that's worth mentioning – workshops and courses where you can learn the neon art by creating your very own work.

Take a Neon Cruise

Once or twice a month, from May to October, MONA offers a Neon Cruise, a night-time tour on a double-decker bus, where clued-up guides give a detailed explanation of the history, decline, and rebirth of these signs across the city, from the banking district to Hollywood.

A captivating, playful and erudite saga far from the overcrowded guided tours that promise to take in the homes of the stars (you mostly get to see massive closed gates).

RUNWAY OF DISUSED GRAND CENTRAL AIR TERMINAL

⑥

A milestone in US aviation history

1310 Air Way, Glendale
Tower can be seen from Grand Central Avenue, site of the former runway

If romantic moviegoers often confuse the disused Grand Central Air Terminal with Van Nuys airport, a few miles northwest, it's because the

control tower is similar to the one in the next-to-last scene of Michael Curtiz' classic film *Casablanca* (1942), starring Humphrey Bogart and Ingrid Bergman.

The same California Mission architecture ("Spanish Colonial Revival") with Art Deco touches, the same arid mountains surrounding the tarmac, the same geographical location in The Valley – we're not in Morocco, but we sure can act like we are! Though some movies have been made at Glendale airport over the years, this former landmark of American aviation is now owned by Disney (under the name "Grand Central Creative Campus," which includes several branches of the "Mouse Factory").

After it opened in the 1920s, Grand Central Air Terminal was LA's main airport for almost 30 years until it was replaced by LAX and, to a lesser extent, Bob Hope Airport in Burbank. Howard Hughes, Amelia Earhart and Charles Lindbergh were just some of the personalities who took off from (or landed on) its runways. In World War II it was used as a training camp for pilots and mechanics, then abandoned for several decades.

Since their renovation, launched in 1999 and completed in 2015, the buildings have showcased many aspects of the entertainment giant. Two hangars have been preserved in addition to the main complex but, to the great regret of aviation enthusiasts, they're not listed on the National Register of Historic Places.

Street that used to be an airport runway

The tarmac was returned to the city as soon as the airport closed. Today, Grand Central Avenue, leading into the Disney campus, is actually one of the runways from which Lockheed P-38 fighters and Boeing B-29 bombers took off. It reverted to a road in 1959.

SOUTH KEYSTONE STREET

⑦

Backlot street

From number 400 to number 599
Freeway CA-134, exit 3

To the north of the sprawling city, along the Los Angeles River, are three of Hollywood's most iconic studios: Universal, Warner Brothers and Walt Disney, from west to east. While the first two easily can be visited via their theme park or organized tour (for a fee), the third has always cultivated a taste for secrecy: unless you're personally acquainted with an employee or invited to a private screening, you're unlikely to be admitted into the lair of the legendary mouse.

By way of consolation, there are Disney theme parks, too, of course – temples of consumption that try to recreate the magic of full-length cartoons, but they are located about 40 miles further south. For a more original and intimate experience at zero cost, away from the hustle and bustle, make your way up to Burbank. There, right up against the all-powerful studio, is the most remarkable street in town. The studio was originally built for animation, but in 1940, after the success of *Snow White and the Seven Dwarfs*, when the studio was looking to expand with the ambition of filming with flesh-and-bone actors and TV productions, it was faced with the most mundane of constraints – a lack of space.

After building sets for indoor scenes, some frontages and offices, there was clearly no room for expansion on the 50 acres that Walt Disney had initially bought. So on completion of the Frank G. Wells Tower, by then entirely given over to animation, the company bought the properties at the south end of South Keystone Street. It is almost identical to the section just north of Alameda Avenue, but you'll never see parked cars except during filming. And for good reason – though the houses are real and not just façades (as is generally the case on backlots), they're empty shells that scenographers and decorators can remodel at will to create suitable spaces. The lawns are visibly greener than in the next street, there's nothing out of place, no trash cans or mailboxes, and the drapes are permanently closed ... But the street is open: it's a public highway and Disney was only able to buy the houses. Park at one end and enjoy the tranquility as you imagine yourself strolling along this straight-as-a-die street in *High School Musical* or *Saving Mr. Banks*.

WALT'S BARN

The only Disney-themed attraction that's free

5202 Zoo Drive
+1 (818) 934-0173
carolwood.org
Third Sunday of each month, 11am–3pm
Admission free

Walt Disney's passion for trains and the railroad has long been illustrated by the distinctive layout of his theme parks, encircled by rails for tourist train rides, like in an autonomous and idealized mini-city. But it doesn't stop there. The former workshop of Mickey's creator – Walt's Barn – maintained by the non-profit Carolwood Foundation, is the finest small-scale example. The barn, open to the public only on the third Sunday of each month, is "the only Disney-themed attraction that's free," according to a volunteer staff member during a fall Sunday visit.

Notably, Disney built a steam railroad that ran through his Los Angeles property, and operated the "Carolwood Pacific Railroad," as it was known, transporting family and friends to the edges of his land.

In the workshop, built in 1950, Disney also spent countless hours controlling the passage of the train, busying himself with railroad models, and dreaming. For many, this barn is considered the birthplace of Imagineering, the company of engineers and architects that designs the legendary parks and hotels with the unmistakable mouse brand.

But don't go looking for the barn at Disney's former property at 355 North Carolwood Drive in Holmby Hills. This quaint red building, an exact replica of one on the family farm in Marceline, Missouri, was moved "behind" Griffith Park, on the San Fernando Valley side, in the late 1990s after the family home was sold. Since then, Walt's daughter has actively contributed to its preservation, with the help of the Carolwood Pacific Historical Society, which endeavors to preserve Disney's railroad legacy.

In this natural setting, you'll find tools, archive images, historical documents, and models, as well as a track control system. This journey through time also reveals the quirks of a creator with all-consuming obsessions, such as building a tunnel by the house to prevent his wife, Lilly, from seeing the steam engine pass by her kitchen windows.

You can discover more by watching the volunteers operate the steam engines, or even take a ride through the park on the little train.

This is a great outing reserved for big kids with a Peter Pan syndrome.

ALFRED HITCHCOCK'S BUNGALOW 5195

⑨

Former offices of the master of suspense

100 Universal City Plaza, Universal City
+1 (800) 864-8377
universalstudioshollywood.com
Metro: Red Line, Universal City stop

Although Universal Studios Hollywood, in the heart of Universal City, is one of LA's most popular tourist destinations, behind the rides and restaurants it's still the working headquarters of many "Dream Factory" enterprises.

Take the Studio Tour (only offered in English, Spanish and Mandarin) to get a glimpse into the secrets of making iconic films and TV series. Façades, offices, film sets, simulations of chases or attacks, all the elements are there. But the attractions are often a letdown as they feel compelled to entertain, constrained by the production teams rushing about behind the scenes, ignoring the trams driving around packed with onlookers.

But there's one discreet and particularly poignant relic that the guides sometimes mention: Alfred Hitchcock's bungalow, which has a history all its own.

Sporting on its façade the distinctive silhouette of the English-born filmmaker who became a US citizen in 1955, Bungalow 5195, as it is known, once housed the offices of the master of suspense.

Hitchcock, while under contract to Hollywood, shot the most successful films of his American career at Universal City (*Psycho*, whose house and motel can also be seen on this tour, was in fact the last film he made with Paramount Pictures, "relocated" to Universal).

The other buildings near the offices were once the home-away-from-home dressing rooms of Rock Hudson and James Stewart, among other big-screen stars. Steven Spielberg's production company (Amblin Entertainment) now has offices in the extension, but it's not signposted.

Now, 60 years later, Universal Cable Productions, which specializes in television, occupies Hitch's rooms and carries his torch, notably by releasing a new DVD collection of his famous *Alfred Hitchcock Presents* series.

Norman Bates house

If you planned to avoid getting caught up in the money-squandering lifestyle of this entertainment capital, but need your Hitchcock fix, make your way to Blair Drive, at the junction with Barham Boulevard, for an unrestricted and unfamiliar view of the house occupied by Norman Bates (and his famous mom), which has moved a few times since 1960. For the less energetic, Hitchcock also has two stars on Hollywood Boulevard's Walk of Fame: one for his contribution to the art of cinema, the other for his television productions.

THE ORIGINAL ROUTE OF THE FIRST CAMPO DE CAHUENGA MISSION

⑩

The discreet birthplace of the State of California

Campo de Cahuenga Memorial Park
3919 Lankershim Boulevard, Studio City
(818) 763-7651 – laparks.org/historic/campo-de-cahuenga
Museum open to the public on the first and third Saturday of the month, 12 noon–4pm, or by appointment only

The Tongva Native American tribe had been living on this tiny patch of land, now hemmed in between Universal Studios, Highway 101 and the Los Angeles River, for nearly 4,000 years before the Spanish settlers, led by Father Fermin de Lausen, built an adobe evangelization mission, from 1795 to 1810, in the parkland known as the Campo de Cahuenga.

Next came the Mexican period, following the War of Independence, which, with the 1821 Treaty of Córdoba, delivered the country from 300 years of Hispanic rule. Finally there was the war that the United States declared on Mexico over a stark issue of compensation – and

© Paula Katherine Marmor

the acquisition of precious territory. So from fierce battles to peace treaties, alliances to betrayals, this "Cahuenga field," where in 1950 the municipality erected a replica of the mission building a few feet from where the original once stood, could be considered the birthplace of the state. This was the site of a series of the most important decisions in Californian history.

On January 13, 1847, it was in the predecessor of this small house-like museum that John C. Frémont (representing the American forces) met with Andrés Pico (representing the Mexicans) to sign the surrender of the "Californios" and draw up the final shape of what would become the 31st State of the Union two years later. Peace was secured by the Treaty of Guadalupe Hidalgo, which at first designated these lost territories as "cessions," but Mexico was later forced to cede them to the US to end the military occupation.

Although the original treaty is housed in the museum, traces of the demolished then rebuilt structure where the birth of "California" was signed can be found represented in the ground. In the adjoining park and surrounding streets, the historic "footprint" of the original foundations is marked by cobblestones. All around the museum, follow the white and gray lines on Lankershim Boulevard, in the park, and even in the metro station (see box), to get a clearer idea of the dimensions of the original Campo de Cahuenga mission.

The foundations of the first Campo de Cahuenga mission were unearthed beneath Lankershim Boulevard during excavations for the LA metro Red Line. The Universal City/Studio City station soberly pays tribute to the historical figures who found shelter there: on the platforms, a modest mosaic in red and orange tones retraces the interlaced destinies of those women and men who fought over the same piece of land, convinced of their territorial rights.

"FREEDOM BOULEVARD" BUILDING BY THIERRY NOIR

(11)

A French artist's playfully political work

Lofts at NoHo Commons, 11136 Chandler Boulevard, North Hollywood
+1 (818) 827-3100
loftsatnoho.com
Metro: Red Line, North Hollywood stop

This is one of the city's most colorful buildings and, luckily, it's located right beside a metro station, which, to the exception of Downtown, is rare enough in Los Angeles to be worth mentioning.

If you'd like to spend a car-free day in the renowned San Fernando Valley, it's easy. The NoHo Arts District, where the Red Line arrives (terminus: North Hollywood station), is a dynamic gateway to this "other LA." Before immersing yourself in the neighborhood, head north past the metro parking lot for a block or so. There, strange characters painted on a white background brighten some of the walls of a modern loft building. The name of the artist, incongruous considering the explosion of color, is there for all to see: Thierry Noir (*noir* is French for black).

This legendary Frenchman began painting his street art on the Berlin Wall in 1984 after moving to Germany. In West Berlin's Kreuzberg district, he was one of the first to challenge this symbol of the Cold War with his sweeping brushstrokes. After a life spent drawing a world of naive, yet instantly recognizable and highly political, characters, his work reached Los Angeles, thanks to a 2009 initiative of the Wende Museum, when an example of his famed Berlin Wall graffiti was exhibited in front of LACMA beside the work of fellow artists (see page 90), on original wall segments moved there for the occasion.

Another authentic segment painted by Thierry Noir can be seen in the Hollywood Hills, and examples of his work dot the city. Apart from a large downtown mural on a black background (in a narrow alley off Spring Street), these tend to be more discreet.

In 2017, a real estate agent from North Hollywood commissioned the artist to paint the entire frontage of a building, an unprecedented area of 15,000 square feet – his largest public mural to date – for the 50th anniversary of the twinning of Los Angeles with Berlin. The result: this sparkling and fun "Freedom Boulevard" which delights passers-by and gives NoHo back its proud colors. The vast residential complex known as "The Valley" had suffered for years from a vaguely tacky reputation as a soulless dormitory, according to the hipster Angelenos settled in Hollywood, Santa Monica, or Los Feliz, i.e. south of Griffith Park. There's a recent revival of interest in The Valley, mainly thanks to the coveted Studio City, a new temple of cool with trendy restaurants and charming houses, perfectly located between the studios and hills.

DONALD C. TILLMAN WATER RECLAMATION PLANT

⑫

For all fans of Star Trek ... and wastewater

6100 Woodley Avenue, Van Nuys
+1 (818) 778-4226
lacitysan.org
Visits by reservation only

Although this isn't the only LA location (from the Getty Center to Griffith Park) to have hosted the various incarnations of the legendary series (and movies) from the *Star Trek* universe, it is by far the most recognizable and impressive.

No wonder: designed by Anthony J. Lumsden and built in 1984, the Donald C. Tillman Water Reclamation Plant, with its obtuse angles and postmodern concrete, is like a spacecraft set in an idyllic natural site. Yet this building was meant to represent the Starfleet Academy, the school for future officers, which is supposedly located in San Francisco (the Golden Gate Bridge was added post-production).

In real life, around 100 million liters of wastewater from the San Fernando Valley pass through the building each day, where it's treated to provide water for irrigation. Watering green spaces (see below), golf courses (abundant in the region) or irrigating agricultural land are all ways to recycle water after biological treatment by nitrification.

However unsexy it may seem at first, you can tour this plant and three others, by reservation only, as part of a very informative (and free) program launched by the City of Los Angeles. The aim is to inform residents about the sewers, sewage and other household waters, starting with the separation of liquids and solids. Solid waste, for example, is sent to the Hyperion Water Reclamation Plant to be processed into a source of energy and fertilizer.

NEARBY

SuihoEn, The Japanese Garden

+1 (818) 756-8166
suihoen.thejapanesegarden.com/new
Monday–Thursday 11am–4 pm, Sunday 10am–4pm

As a showcase for the adjacent water treatment plant, the astonishing SuihoEn ("Garden of Water and Fragrance"), designed by landscape architect and artist Koichi Kawana, was opened at the same time to prove that such a place could also be a healthy sanctuary. Cherry trees, magnolias, lotus, and a hundred other plant and tree species share the limelight in this Chisen-Kaiyushiki (the term for a "wet-strolling" garden). Waterfalls, lakes, streams, and a teahouse complete the perfect picture of what is surely the most beautiful and relaxing of the region's Japanese gardens. A sure favorite.

DOOR TO ROOM A113 OF CALARTS

⑬

The A113 mystery

California Institute of the Arts
24700 McBean Parkway
Valencia
+1 (661) 255-1050
calarts.edu
Campus open year-round

This must be the best-known "Easter Egg" (a hidden reference or inside joke that some directors discreetly feature in their work) in recent American productions.

The next time you take in a movie by Disney, Pixar, or one of their affiliates (Lucas Films, Marvel, etc.), watch for this: at some point a mysterious letter "A" will inevitably appear, followed by the number "113."

Omnipresent in animations, this "A113" leaves fans hysterical and conspiracy theorists wary. Is this an Illuminati sign, the mark of a secret society destined to dominate the world, the path to a parallel dimension, an encrypted message? Or just a kids' joke?

But why, if so, is this "A113" so ubiquitous, from a license plate in *Toy Story* to a brand of camera in *Finding Nemo* and a label in *Ratatouille*, not to mention appearances in productions like *The Simpsons*, *Hunger Games* and *Mission: Impossible*?

The answer is more trivial than you'd think, and can be found in Valencia, about an hour's drive north of LA.

When Walt Disney planned to open a private university for the creative arts in 1961, he first merged two art schools before building a huge main facility on an isolated lot in the Santa Clarita hills. To the north, all the gravity of a campus hidden in the woods and to the south, at Anaheim, quite the opposite – an amusement park given over to families and consumerism. Midway between the two lies the sprawling City of Los Angeles with its myriad artists and fertile brains buzzing around Burbank Studios. A perfect straight line, marked out by Highway 5.

Generations of students following their artistic calling to create or even direct the Hollywood studios (including Sofia Coppola and Tim Burton, among others) have graced the halls of CalArts (the nickname for the California Institute of the Arts), which is dedicated to the study of dance, cinema, literature and theater as well as the visual arts.

Brad Bird, future director of *The Incredibles*, was one of them, as were Pete Docter, Andrew Stanton, and John Lasseter, who became artistic director of Pixar Animation Studios and Walt Disney Animation Studio. These four would revolutionize the cartoon world.

Brad Bird launched the joke in 1989 as a nod to room A113, where these movie craftsmen studied graphics and character animation. To the delight of obsessional fans, several studios are perpetuating the tradition. This magical and certainly lucky number still figures on the door of the beloved room.

The campus is worth a detour for anyone heading to San Francisco, especially since rumor has it that *Star Wars: The Empire Strikes Back* was partly filmed in the modular theater. An engineering marvel, it is said to have hosted the mythical scene of filial revelation between Darth Vader and Luke Skywalker.

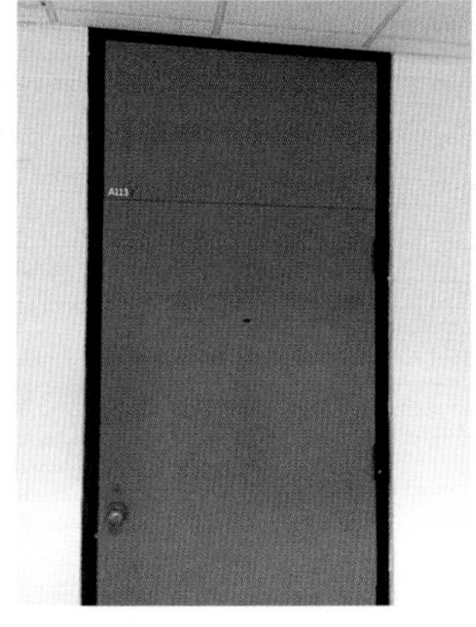

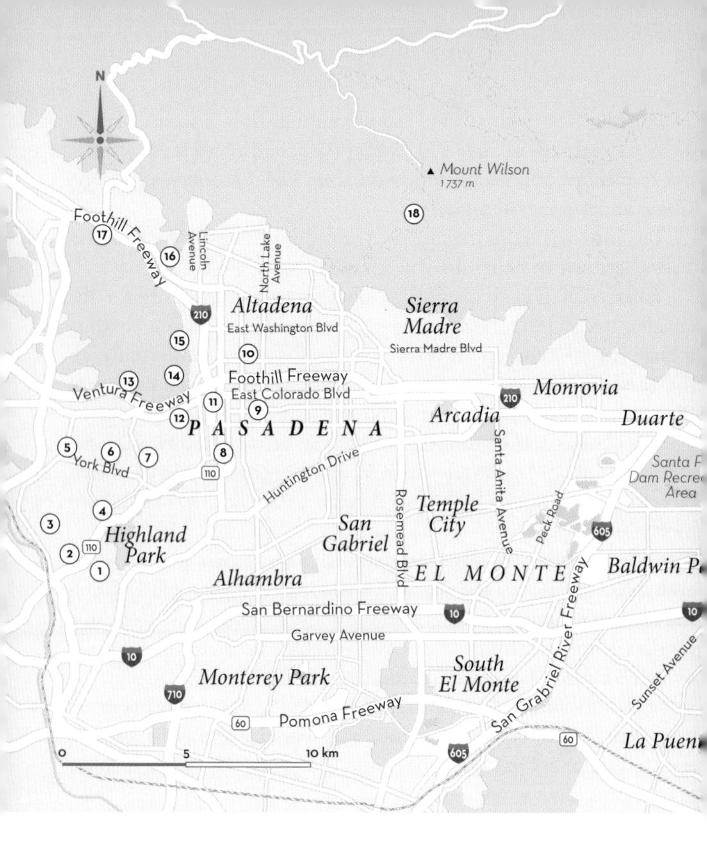

Pasadena and East

① HERITAGE SQUARE MUSEUM 166
② LUMMIS HOME (EL ALISAL) 168
③ SELF-REALIZATION FELLOWSHIP LAKE SHRINE 170
④ CHICKEN BOY 172
⑤ MOORE LABORATORY OF ZOOLOGY 174
⑥ LOS ANGELES POLICE MUSEUM 176
⑦ CHURCH OF THE ANGELS BELL 178
⑧ SECRETS OF PASADENA'S GIANT FORK 180
⑨ HIDDEN IN THE HAIR OF JACKIE AND MACK ROBINSON 182
⑩ BUNGALOW HEAVEN NEIGHBORHOOD 184
⑪ ARMENIAN GENOCIDE MEMORIAL TEARS 186

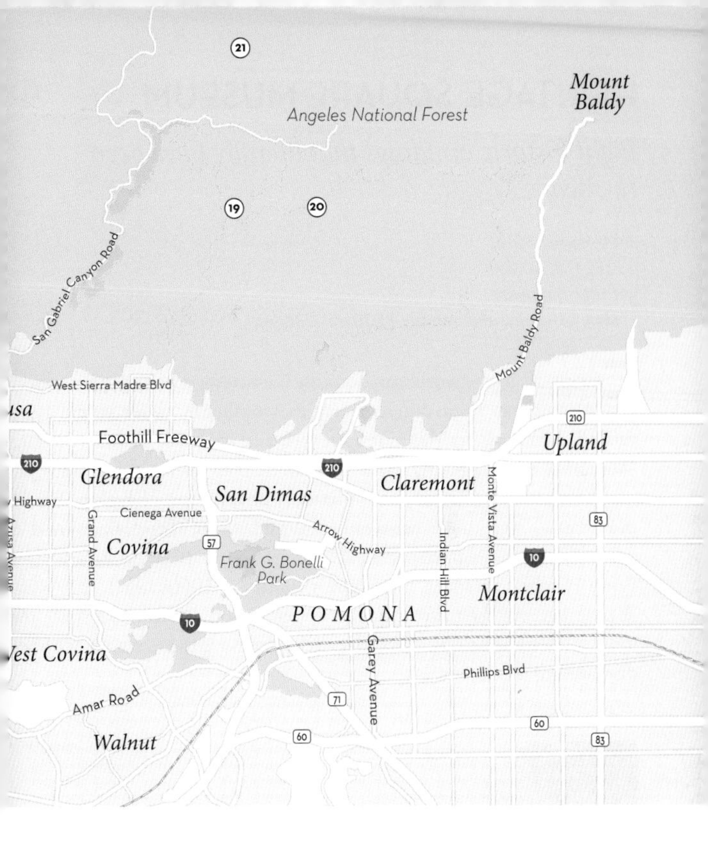

⑫ COLORADO STREET SUICIDE BRIDGE 188

⑬ EAGLE ROCK 190

⑭ FINNISH FOLK ART MUSEUM – PASADENA MUSEUM OF HISTORY 192

⑮ THE GAMBLE HOUSE 194

⑯ "DEVIL'S GATE" DAM 196

⑰ ANCIENT FOREST IN DESCANSO GARDENS 198

⑱ MOUNT WILSON OBSERVATORY 200

⑲ BRIDGE TO NOWHERE HIKE 202

⑳ MOUNT BALDY ZEN CENTER 204

㉑ REMAINS OF THE "SOCIALIST COLONY" OF THE LLANO DEL RIO COLLECTIVE 206

HERITAGE SQUARE MUSEUM

①

Eight historic buildings that literally have been re-sited

3800 Homer Street
+1 (323) 225-2700
heritagesquare.org
Friday, Saturday, and Sunday 11:30am–4:30pm

Few places in the world can boast such a heterogeneous concentration of buildings from different eras that ordinarily never would have rubbed shoulders. Yet this is the strength and charm of Heritage Square Museum, strictly speaking less a museum than an open-air time warp.

These mansions, with their Victorian architecture of highly diverse provenance, were built between 1850 and 1950. They all enjoyed a peaceful life in their respective LA neighborhoods (Lincoln Heights, Boyle Heights, Pasadena, Downtown) until the 1960s, when they were abandoned and then threatened with demolition. So to make space for more modern buildings, it was decided ... to move them, whole, without dismantling them!

Entire homes traveled on huge trailers to Highland Park where, right next to the highway – the ultimate anachronism – they now reflect a bygone era. To complete the effect, the museum guides are even dressed in period costume.

The museum was created on the initiative of the Cultural Heritage Foundation of Southern California, a non-profit organization and fundraiser, "to preserve, collect and interpret the architecture, physical environment, and culture of Southern California during the first 100 years of statehood," as its slogan says.

Hale House is arguably the most iconic of all, with its pale green walls and brick-lined tower, but the eight historically significant buildings each have unique features: here the simplicity of the Octagon House, elsewhere the opulence of the William Perry Mansion, there a church, there again a beautifully restored pharmacy.

Despite the mix of genres, the idea was to recreate a village atmosphere, middle-class as it is, with an "uptown" residential area and a "downtown" commercial district. Although the result may be rather less realistic and vibrant than the original vision of these history buffs, each of the eight is individually spectacular.

LUMMIS HOME (EL ALISAL)

②

A stone castle hand-built by a lone man

200 East Avenue 43
laparks.org/historic/lummis-home-and-gardens
mota.dreamhosters.com/lummis-home-and-garden
Saturday and Sunday 10am–3pm
Admission free

Charles Fletcher Lummis, a *Los Angeles Times* reporter who turned his back on Cincinnati to settle in LA, made his way cross-country on foot while chronicling his trip with weekly dispatches to the newspaper. On arrival, he was offered the more sedentary post of

city editor covering local news, and built himself a home on the banks of the Arroyo Seco with stones he dragged from the riverbed, which was dry at the time.

The result of his superhuman effort, completed around 1910, is regularly referred to as a "castle" by connoisseurs. Not only does this impressive building reflect its owner's eccentric personality, it resembles a hermit's refuge with its little tower and low doors. "El Alisral" ("The Sycamore"), as Lummis named his home after the giant tree nearby, prefigured the Arts and Crafts esthetic that became fashionable a few years later. The floor was concrete, the furniture wood, with some finely carved pieces, and large beams spanned the living room ceiling. The features seen today are almost all original.

Once his home was ready, Lummis, who was very close to nature without rejecting the worldly life of the city and became known as a historian, ethnographer, photographer, and activist for Native American rights, invited artists and intellectuals, musicians, and dancers to reputedly extravagant gatherings.

On his death, the house was bequeathed to the Southwest Museum, which sold it to the State of California before the city took possession. You can now visit on the weekend and see photos of the construction work, as well as superb stained-glass windows depicting indigenous communities, created by Lummis himself using his own vintage shots. Stand in the central courtyard, between the main house and guest house, for a clear impression of the influence of another type of architecture: the Mission Revival style that defines the whole property, especially its colonnaded patio. The gardens are filled with California desert native plants and sycamore trees.

SELF-REALIZATION FELLOWSHIP LAKE SHRINE ③

One of the most enchanting sites around

17190 Sunset Boulevard
lakeshrine.org
310-454-4114
Wednesday–Sunday noon–4pm
Reservations taken via website at 10am Saturday for the following week
Ceremonies in the temple: Discontinued during Covid

Autobiography of a Yogi, published in 1946, is considered one of the most important spiritual books of the 20th century. It was written by Paramahansa Yogananda, who in the 1920s traveled across the US teaching the precepts of Kriya Yoga philosophy through his Self-Realization Fellowship. In 1950, he founded a haven of peace in exquisite taste at Pacific Palisades, perhaps the most enchanting site in the region.

This sublime location, very popular with certain Western musicians and businessmen drawn to Indian mysticism (like Elvis Presley, Steve Jobs, and even George Harrison, who married there), is an invitation to refoçus on yourself and commune with nature. A lake embellished with several temples, a windmill chapel and a luxuriant garden, among other curiosities such as a houseboat, call for meditation and understanding between religions (a concept interpreted by a poignant monument).

Even rarer, a small Chinese sarcophagus surrounded by flowers and topped with a pergola shelters some of the ashes of Gandhi, the Indian leader and spiritual guide, who wanted his remains to be dispersed in different rivers around the planet.

Yogananda, as his friend, received some of the ashes in Los Angeles, shortly after the Mahatma's assassination. Although this site didn't need to summon up such a historical figure to be fascinating, Ghandi's presence only accentuates its magical aura.

Shumei Hollywood Center

7406 Franklin Avenue
Metro: Red Line, Hollywood / Highland stop
Gardens can be visited on request
+1 (323) 876-5528

The Shumei spiritual organization ("World Messianic Church" in Europe, sometimes considered a sect) was founded in the 1930s by the Japanese philosopher Mokichi Okada. In Hollywood, a handsome house in an indeterminate style (Greek columns, Spanish façade, French windows) serves as its center. The house once belonged to writer and journalist Joan Didion and has seen everything that Hollywood and American rock has to offer, from drugs to high spirits. Seemingly purged of demons, it's now an oasis where patients come to treat their spiritual or physical afflictions, through Jyorei workshops and other exercises inspired by a mixture of Shintoism, Buddhism, and Christianity. Tea ceremonies, arts performances, and festivals also are held here.

CHICKEN BOY

④

A 22-foot human chicken statue, relic of Route 66

5558 North Figueroa Street
+1 (323) 254-4565
chickenboy.com
futurestudio.typepad.com
Always visible from the street
Metro: Gold Line, Highland Park stop

With no Statue of Liberty worthy of the name, LA residents, who have always known how to cultivate eccentricity, have a 22 foot human chicken statue, which was saved from imminent destruction when an art director spotted it on Broadway (downtown) and had it installed on her gallery roof.

But according to the official website, set up with the emerging cult of the bird with red tee and yellow bucket, the story goes back to the 1960s.

At the time, the statue merely promoted the skills of a fiberglass company, before the grilled chicken restaurant that gave him his name replaced the boy's face with a bird's head. So, like other unusual monuments along the iconic route, this became one of the essential stops on Route 66, which at the time passed through the city (see page 124).

In 2007, Amy Inouye, now known as "Chicken Boy's mom," installed the structure on the roof of her creative "Future Studio," which is also an art gallery, in Highland Park, north of downtown. "In 1984, when I realized that the restaurant had closed, I got the phone number of the leasing agent to inquire about the future of the statue. He finally called me back saying that because of the work at the site, Chicken Boy had to come down. 'If you're so concerned about him, come and get him,' " she told the press in 2007. He was listed as historic heritage in 2010, thanks to California Gov. Arnold Schwarzenegger.

Like any obscure cult dedicated to an iconic figure of a totally random place, its popularity is quite relative, and only a few offbeat hipsters and Route 66 fanatics can boast about the existence and current location of the chicken, which may have gained visibility in recent years with the revival of Highland Park, now trending.

Like Silverlake's "Happy Foot / Sad Foot" sign (see page 70), the cult has given rise to an online souvenir shop, managed by the studio, where you can buy Chicken Boy badges, soft toys, and assorted mugs.

MOORE LABORATORY OF ZOOLOGY

⑤

The shimmering colors of a unique collection of birds

Occidental College
1600 Campus Road / Bird Road
moorelab.oxy.edu
+1 (323) 259-2500 – +1 (323) 259-1352
Visits by reservation only

In the heart of a small private college nestled in the hills of Eagle Rock district (where Barack Obama studied for two years), an incredible zoology laboratory has over the years listed 65,000 bird specimens, now stuffed (including almost 7,000 hummingbirds), 1,300 skeletons, over 500 preserved eggs and a number of nests, as well as a small mammal collection.

Robert T. Moore, born 1882, was an ornithologist who traveled across the Americas to document the genetic makeup of a multitude of bird species, amassing one of the largest collections in the world. In 1934 he undertook the compilation of the first complete list of Mexico's endemic birds, a vocation that occupied him for the rest of his life. Before he died in 1958, Moore donated his impressive collections and several buildings to Occidental College, founded in 1887.

Today, the laboratory that bears his name (known as MLZ), integrated into the college's Department of Biology, uses these specimens to study ornithological evolution over the course of history, with particular attention given to the environmental impact on the geographic distribution, biodiversity, appearance, and DNA of birds. Through their website you can book a tour of the laboratory, where teachers and technicians enthusiastically welcome anyone keen to know more about their specialty and the characteristics of the birds, some of which are over a hundred years old.

Dozens of wooden trays showcase an impressive variety of shapes, beaks, and iridescent plumes, all labeled with the name of the species in Latin, sex, date, and origin. Their characteristics are sometimes very similar, and the rows of birds show such an astonishing range of bright colors you'd think they were a still-life painting. A real favorite that combines erudition with a sensation of opening the door to a secret world.

Pasadena's wild parrots

There is an urban myth that in the 1960s, a fire in a Pasadena pet store released into the wild several birds representing a dozen species from eastern Mexico (where they are listed as endangered). Since then, they have reproduced prolifically and firmly established themselves in the region. Sometimes in Pasadena you only need look up into the trees to see them, especially in spring.

LOS ANGELES POLICE MUSEUM

⑥

LAPD: four myth-making letters

6045 York Boulevard
(323) 344-9445
laphs.org
Tuesday–Friday 10am– 4pm, and third Saturday of the month 9am–3pm
Metro: Gold Line, Highland Park Station stop

The Los Angeles Police Museum is housed in Highland Park Police Station, the city's oldest surviving police station, so it's breathtakingly realistic.

But on entering the 1926 neo-Renaissance building (restored and now listed as a Historic Cultural Monument), you still don't expect to

see the jail cells nor the little reception desk so characteristic of American police stations. "Number 11," as it's known, was closed for some 20 years before the Los Angeles Police Historical Society (LAPHS) decided to rehabilitate it to display vehicles, artifacts, and documents.

LAPD: four letters forming one of the most iconic acronyms in American culture and law enforcement, a legend in themselves. The famous midnight-blue wool uniforms are displayed upstairs with certain pride, while in the next room archives of the most sordid and high-profile cases are lined up, making your head spin. The gruesome discovery of the "Black Dahlia" in 1947, murders perpetrated by the Manson "family" in 1969, the Black Panthers shooting in 1974, the misdeeds of the Skid Row Slasher in 1975, the assassination of Nicole Brown Simpson in 1994 – a virtual goldmine of crime and name-dropping, which has so inspired writers and directors from Raymond Chandler to James Ellroy and Billy Wilder.

In the inner courtyard sit squad cars, helicopters, and even tanks, as if laid to rest after a life of chases and riots in one of the most crime-ridden and policed cities in the States.

Police Academy cafe: dinner with the cops, open to the public

On the grounds of the LA Police Academy near Dodger Stadium, the Los Angeles Police Revolver and Athletic Club Cafe, 1880 North Academy Drive, reopened in 2014 after a much-needed renovation.

Surprising it may be, but in this unlikely place you really can smell the coffee, taste the eggs and pancakes among the boys (and gals) in blue — new recruits, hardened cops and detectives — all on black fake-leather benches and surrounded by archival photos. It's quite a trip. However, although open to the public (6am–2pm only, Monday–Friday), all this can be rather intimidating, and few people dare visit.

To find it, go through the security check, take the outside steps, then walk to the end of the path on the right until you see the stone façade.

CHURCH OF THE ANGELS BELL

⑦

English countryside in Pasadena

1100 Avenue 64, Pasadena
+1 (323) 255-3878
coa-pasadena.org
Church open year-round; Sunday Mass at 7:45am and 10:15am

The highway interchanges and palm trees reaching for the sky might just seem like a momentary mirage. At the turn of an avenue appears another type of exhilarating landmark, a building with a bell tower piercing the blue. The oldest church in Pasadena also seems to be the most out of place, with its forms more reminiscent of English churches than any local architectural style.

Built in 1889 for Frances Campbell-Johnston, in memory of her late husband, diplomat Alexander Robert Campbell-Johnston, Church of the Angels is built on land that was originally the family ranch, San Rafael – at a time, it goes without saying, when this part of southern California was studded with farms.

British architect Arthur Edmund Street drew up the plans, which were adapted by Ernest Albert Coxhead, who designed a dozen churches for Los Angeles. Apart from the earthquake-damaged tower, the elements of this building are original.

Although a bell still rings from the tower, the one near the entrance has a special and more intimate tale to tell: originally located at the heart of the ranch, it was used to call the residents and employees at mealtimes – so nothing religious, until the property owner died. Afterward, the sound of the bell became more invasive and the new building was used as a place of worship in the village of Garvanza, a stone's throw south on the banks of the Arroyo Seco River.

The church, vandalized in 2017 by graffiti artists and attempted arson, has already regained its former splendor thanks to its very active and dedicated community.

Sunday morning Mass is still celebrated, as well as weddings, both real and fictional. As Hollywood is attracted by the impeccable esthetics, numerous TV series and movies have been shot here.

At any moment it seems that a fairytale princess and her Prince Charming could emerge from the Storybook architecture.

Whether admiring the organ and altar inside, or the details of the Gothic Revival influences outside, a visit is an enchantment highlighted by the "anachronistic geography."

Outside, in a landscaped heart-shaped garden with stone sundial, the eponymous angel bears a cross on his back and watches, patiently. The vast memorial window, designed and made for the church by the London firm of Cox & Buckley, is one of the most spectacular in the country.

SECRETS OF PASADENA'S GIANT FORK ⑧

A tasteful birthday present

"Fork Plaza," 200 Bellenfontaine,
Pasadena
pasadenasforkintheroad.blogspot.com
coffeegallery.com

Word play on the meanings of "fork" led to the installation of a fun, 18-foot-tall sculpture, without the agreement of the Pasadena authorities. Separating South Pasadena Avenue and South St. John Avenue, the fork now stands proudly on its own plot, survivor of a serious legal entanglement with the city. It must be said that Bob Stane, to whom this impromptu implement originally paid tribute, is an extraordinary figure. Mainstay of the local folk (fork?) scene, promoter of many talented performers at an age when others would be retiring, he founded a music venue with incredible charm – the Coffee Gallery Backstage (in Altadena, north of Pasadena). In a few years, it became one of the must-see places around.

In 2009, artist Ken Marshall made this object in wood, painted in metallic colors, as a 75th birthday present for his friend, Stane. A small team of admirers disguised as road workers dug a hole overnight to plant the bulky sculpture, anchored in a concrete slab and supported by a wooden frame. The surprise was short-lived because a few months later the fork disappeared from the intersection, on the orders of City Hall. After the necessary permission was finally obtained, the fork reappeared in 2011 as a focal point for charity drives and "good food" events.

Bob Stane's path, like his giant fork and intersection, hasn't run in a straight line either. Before the music venue adventure and its culinary tribute, his best-known and recognized achievement was the legendary Ice House, a comedy club he opened with Willard Chilcott in 1960 in Pasadena. Here a generation of artists was discovered, from David Letterman to Jay Leno, Tom Waits to Steve Martin. Enough to whet the LA appetite for the absurd, at least as absurd as this fork planted at a fork in the road.

HIDDEN IN THE HAIR OF JACKIE AND MACK ROBINSON

⑨

Follow the gaze of the two athletes ... close up on their Afros

Jackie and Mack Robinson Memorial
101 Garfield Avenue

Two brothers raised in Pasadena, alumni of John Muir High School and the local college. Two exceptional athletes. Two diverging destinies ...

Jackie Robinson, a tireless civil rights activist, went down in history for breaking the color barrier in Major League Baseball on April 15, 1947, when he debuted for the Brooklyn Dodgers. He originally was signed for the Montreal Royals by the club's general manager Branch Rickey while still playing for the Kansas City Monarchs in the Negro

Leagues. In this way, the club put an end to decades of racial segregation in the sport. Since 2004, the MLB has paid tribute to him every April 15, celebrating "Jackie Robinson Day."

Although Matthew "Mack" Robinson was less well-known and celebrated than his younger brother, he won the silver medal – under the gaze of Adolf Hitler – in the men's 200 meters at the 1936 Berlin Olympics. He finished four-tenths of a second behind the undisputed hero of the course, Jesse Owens. Back in Pasadena, he strove to lower the city's crime rate.

The handsome memorial that has honored the brothers since 1997 consists of two imposing statues representing their faces, each looking in a different direction. Jackie is gazing east towards Brooklyn, the New York borough where he spent most of his career. Mack's eyes are riveted on City Hall, because he never left Pasadena.

At first glance, there's nothing exceptional about the bronze sculptures. About 9 feet high, the brothers appear calm and solemn. A nearby information board introduces them simply. But sculptors Ralph Helmick and John Outterbridge intentionally etched into the athletes' bronze hair many highlights of their lives, with drawings and anecdotes that can only be seen at close range.

Approaching their apparently "smooth" Afros you'll discover, hidden in their metallic hair, an interweaving of tiny details describing their lives in the manner of tattoos, or an intimate bas-relief. Their main achievements, significant dates, political commitments, speeches and other iconic images of sporting feats overlap on the two bronze skulls. Hidden within a tribute to the city, the artwork is a moving way of recording the sometimes veiled and surreptitious struggles for equal rights waged both on and off the sports field by Jackie and Mack Robinson.

On April 15, 1917, another statue of Jackie Robinson was unveiled near LA's Dodger Stadium, to celebrate the 70th anniversary of his first pro match. In fact, the Dodgers franchise moved from New York to LA in 1957 and Jackie was able to come "home" to end his career. The bronze statue, lifesize this time, shows the athlete in full action, stealing a base.

BUNGALOW HEAVEN NEIGHBORHOOD

⑩

A concentration of 800 Arts and Crafts houses

Bungalow Heaven, Pasadena
District bounded by East Washington Boulevard to the north, Orange Grove Boulevard to the south, North Lake Avenue to the west and North Hill Avenue to the east
+1 (626) 585-2172
bungalowheaven.org
Streets accessible year-round
Homes open to the public one day a year, usually in April (check website)
Metro: Gold Line, Lake Station stop

In central Pasadena, a stone's throw from Highway 210, is a very special neighborhood made up of 800 homes, each more delectable than

the next, which bears its name like a charm: Bungalow Heaven. Most of the homes in this "paradise" of tree-lined shady streets are historic bungalows with common features, all built in the early 20th century in the Arts and Crafts style so recognizable in California.

This architectural movement emphasized harmony with nature, using mainly wood and stone, flying in the face of the rampant industrialization of the period.

Wide verandas, rows of pillars, open floor plans, porches with cozy eaves (often at street level), and sloping chalet-like roofs characterize this style, which finds its all-American avatar at The Ahwahnee Hotel (formerly The Majestic Yosemite Hotel), in the heart of Yosemite National Park. Also known as National Park Service rustic or Parkitecture, the architectural style is more reminiscent of mountain than desert. Wood and other natural materials are widely used, with the interiors featuring many built-ins, including cabinets, shelving, and seating integrated into the design.

It's been over a decade since the Bungalow Heaven district was listed on the National Register of Historic Places, with a plaque marking the spot, after becoming Pasadena's first "Landmark District" in 1989. But the 16 blocks, with their obvious historical interest, are above all a haven of peace for the residents, who benefit from a quasi-village life and a strong sense of community. Their corner of paradise is regularly cited among the top 10 places to live in America.

ARMENIAN GENOCIDE MEMORIAL TEARS

⑪

One teardrop every 21 seconds

162–172 East Walnut Street, Pasadena

With a community of over one million people in the United States (the second largest diaspora after Russia), the small Caucasian country of Armenia is strongly represented in Southern California, especially in the San Fernando Valley north of Los Angeles. Almost 40% of the 200,000 residents of Glendale are of Armenian origin, the greatest concentration in the world next to the Armenian capital Yerevan (population 1 million). Many of these people are descended from families who crossed the Atlantic in the early 20th century to escape Turkish persecution.

Though not as impressive as the 75-foot concrete tower inaugurated at Montebello in 1968 (about 18 miles further south), the 2015 Pasadena genocide memorial, spearheaded by a dedicated committee, also commemorates the death of the 1.5 million Armenians killed by the Ottomans, led by the nationalist Young Turks movement, between 1915 and 1923.

The sculpture, a metal tripod at the edge of Memorial Park near the Levitt Pavilion, stands like a beacon over a well into which a drop of water falls from the tip every 21 seconds – symbolizing, over a year's time, one tear for each of the missing 1.5 million Armenians. Every April 24, families gather in front of the monument to honor the memory of the victims, a large majority of whom (women and children) were sent to concentration camps in the Syrian desert, only to die of hunger and heat. Their US descendants are still fighting for the Turkish government to recognize the organized massacres of Armenians, as many nations around the world have done.

While fairly private until recently, the memorial is now widely signposted along Highway 210, an initiative approved by the California Senate in 2017.

COLORADO STREET SUICIDE BRIDGE

⑫

100 deaths in a century

504 West Colorado Boulevard, Pasadena
Colorado Street is now Colorado Boulevard
To reach the bridge, take the Orange Grove exit on Highway 134, head south and turn onto Green Street and then Grand Street
There's a small shady park in a dead end where you can leave the car and walk to the bridge
It's illegal to stop a car on the bridge

The Colorado Street Bridge, a grandiose structure that for a few years was part of the legendary Route 66, straddles the Arroyo Seco River between Old Town Pasadena and the Eagle Rock district. With its 150-foot Beaux-Arts arches and characteristic lighting, the imposing 1912 construction is designated a Historic Civil Engineering Landmark.

Over the years, however, it has acquired a curious reputation, pushing local authorities to erect a security barrier, which partly blocks the view but more importantly stops jumpers – in theory.

Although many places around the world have an infamous "suicide bridge" where, mysteriously (or to ensure a successful final bow), locals choose to die, the Colorado Street bridge has seen a terrifying suicide rate ever since the 1930s.

A hundred contenders have hurled themselves to certain death, the first in 1919, then another 50 between 1933 and 1937 (during the Great Depression), until the drama of 2008, when a man who'd stabbed his ex-wife and grandmother jumped, determined to end his life.

Despite the barrier, dating from 1993, the nickname has stuck. Of course, stories grew of ghosts and spirits that supposedly haunt the bridge, re-enacting their leap into the void and scaring passers-by and the homeless out of their minds.

Below, in the shadow of the huge concrete pillars, the neighborhood of opulent houses gives an impression of quiet luxury but also of strangeness. Drive through at dusk after checking out the bridge. Chill factor guaranteed.

But the City of Pasadena, taking to heart the repeated suicides (sometimes several in a few months), has had a plaque installed at the bridge entrance that reads "There is hope," followed by a dedicated emergency number to aid residents with dark thoughts.

EAGLE ROCK

⑬

United States national bird, carved in the rock by nature

5499 Eagle Rock View Drive

Eagle Rock, the LA neighborhood sandwiched between the cities of Glendale and Pasadena, isn't just a quiet dormitory where families like to raise their children (with creeping gentrification, like its Highland Park neighbor). Nor just the home of the magnificent Occidental College, perched in the hills (where a certain Barack Obama spent a couple of years). This northeastern district is for a very obvious reason named after the majestic eagle-shaped rock that can be seen from California State Route 2.

The creature, as if carved from the rock, appears to take flight in various ways depending on the play of light. At certain times of day, you can almost make out a complete head in profile. At other times, depending on the projected shadows, the outstretched wings can be seen on the side of the rock. There was already an interest in such rock formations toward the end of the 19th century, when Ludwig Salvator, Archduke of Austria, first sketched the geologic formation that Spanish colonists called the Piedra Gorda ("Huge Rock"). "The Piedra Gorda, towering above, is an imposing rock of granite conglomerates, on one side with parallel strata having two sharply defined hollows in which swallows have built their nests," he noted in an account of his explorations published in German.

It wasn't until 1996 that the City of Los Angeles took over the rock, which has since become a playground for hikers and climbers. Eagle Rock Canyon Trail, a hiking loop opened in 2006, offers expansive views of the area, on a clear day taking in Catalina Island, Palos Verdes, Hollywood, and downtown. And who knows, from this rock you might spot the iconic bald eagle, better known as the "American eagle," the U.S. national bird. On the endangered list for years, these birds have recently reappeared in Southern California. Dozens of them were seen in the urban environment during the winter of 2017, migrating from the northerly states to regional lakes.

FINNISH FOLK ART MUSEUM – PASADENA MUSEUM OF HISTORY

⑭

Tour within a tour

470 West Walnut Street, Pasadena
pasadenahistory.org/tours/finnish-folk-art-museum
finlandiafoundation.org
+1 (626) 577-1660
Only one guided tour per day of Fenyes Mansion, Friday–Sunday at 12:15pm (approximate duration: 1h15)
Admission fee
Ticket includes the mansion and current exhibition tours: sometimes need to ask the guides to visit the adjoining Folk Art Museum
Closed on public holidays and the day after Thanksgiving

Appearances are very often misleading in LA. After parking among the trees in front of the bucolic entrance to the Pasadena Museum of History, you would expect the Museum of Finnish Folk Art to be a little wooden cabin with sauna and authentic artifacts representative of former immigrants. So when the volunteer guide, Andrea Sossin Bergman, leads you into what is more like a replica of the White House that apparently once belonged to a New York businesswoman and a Hungarian entomoloist who met in Egypt, you're left a bit bewildered. All is explained when you learn that the entrance ticket first gives access to the Fenyes Mansion, a neoclassical Beaux-Arts residence which in 1970 became a museum dedicated to the city of Pasadena and the San Gabriel Valley. Built in 1906 by Robert Farquhar for Eva Scott and her husband Adalbert Fenyes, this sublime structure in the local "Millionaires' Row" contains antique furnishings from all over the world and paintings that are things of beauty.

And Finland in all this?

The couple's granddaughter, Leonora, known as "Babsie," was a linguist who spent time among indigenous peoples. In 1946, she married Yrjo A. Paloheima, a Finnish diplomat who became the Scandinavian country's first consul in Southern California. The mansion, after doubling as the Consulate for 16 years, reverted to a quasi-normal family home for the couple and their four adopted Finnish children. The children later donated the house to the city of Pasadena.

Meanwhile, in 1949, Consul Paloheimo, pining for his homeland, had decided to purchase and relocate a Swiss-like chalet used as a garage by American politician Arthur Flemming. He added a sauna and turned it into a guesthouse, looking after the garden himself and amassing rustic countryside objects during his travels back home.

The consul also set up the Finlandia Foundation, which to this day maintains this charming and modest house/museum, which can be visited as part of the tour. A stone's throw from the grand main property, it holds many traditional Finnish tools and utensils, everyday outfits and carpets made by local artisans. In the center of the living room, with its hand-carved chairs, is a Finnish open fireplace or *takka*, with metal supports where bread and meat can be dried.

The contrast of this slice of ordinary life with the opulence of the adjoining mansion is quite striking. Note: a visit to the Finnish museum is not automatically included, as most visitors only want to see the Fenyes Mansion. Just say you're interested in the little Folk Art Museum, and the guides will be happy to show your small group around.

THE GAMBLE HOUSE

(15)

A moment of beauty that transcends the monotony of life

4 Westmoreland Place, Pasadena
www.gamblehouse.org
+1 (626) 793-3334
Tuesday 10:30am–1pm, Thursday, Friday and Saturday 11:40am–3pm, Sunday 12 noon–3 pm; closed Monday and Wednesday
"Brown Bag Tuesdays" when you can bring your own meal, eat on the terrace and, at 12:30pm, take a 20-minute guided tour
Metro: Gold Line, Memorial Park stop

Masterpiece alert! The Gamble House in Pasadena is far and away the best testimony to the natural architecture of the Craftsman era, inspired by American national parks and a reaction to early 20th-century industrialization with its ubiquitous metal.

This fine mansion, handcrafted in rich woods, is a much less accessible, middle-class and lavish version of the charming little neighborhood of

Bungalow Heaven built in the same style (see page 184), and totally unmissable. "A moment of beauty that transcends the monotony of life," as described by fans of the architectural style, this gem on a grassy knoll overlooking the Arroyo Seco was designed in 1908 by local architects Charles and Henry Greene for David Gamble (heir to the Procter & Gamble household products empire).

Walls, windows, and architectural details are covered in typical artisan representations of leaves, branches, flowers, and insects. Japanese influences also can be seen in the compositions of beams, leaded-glass windows, and lanterns that embellish the interiors. The impressive and original staircase alone is worth a visit. The terrace, open to all on Tuesdays, is ideal for an alfresco lunch.

In 1966, as soon as a horrified Cecil Gamble got wind of the fact that a potential buyer was considering painting over the teak and adding touches of white to the structure, he took the house off the market and donated it to the City of Pasadena and the USC (University of Southern California) school of architecture.

He did good.

© Cullen328

"DEVIL'S GATE" DAM

The road to hell, as the saying goes

Devil's Gate
123 Oak Grove Drive, La Cañada Flintridge
From Hahamongna Park (where you can leave the car), walk south toward the freeway, then go down the steps from the bridge. Turn right at the bottom and follow the creek through the undergrowth that often blocks the way. You're there. The tunnel is no longer open, but the devil's face can still be seen at the entrance.

You don't need a vivid imagination to spot the devil's profile when you walk to the bottom of this abandoned dam wedged between Pasadena and La Cañada Flintridge. Sculpted ears, feral nose, protruding chin, sunken eyes, and prominent horns, it's all there in the heart of the rock. But this place isn't just the birthplace of a large, vaguely frightening anthropomorphic bit of stone.

The dam that sprawls above was built in the 1920s. A few decades later it became a meeting place for a group of occultists spearheaded by LA's most famous, Ron Hubbard, the controversial founder of Scientology. This pseudo-scientific technique of personal development ("Dianetics") became a religious movement around 1953.

From the tunnel that passes under the road (now barred off), Hubbard and his disciples organized spiritualism seances in the hope of reanimating an antichrist figure. Centuries ago, the Tongva Native Americans had already attributed spirit-of-coyote powers to the echo of water flowing in this gorge.

No need for more chilling stories for the place to take on a permanently haunted and accursed atmosphere. For some believers, Hubbard even opened up the gates of hell here. The legend of this "devil's door" was reinforced around 1950, when several children went missing not far from the dam. Not until another 13 years had passed did Mack Ray Edwards, serial killer and road mender who was wreaking havoc around the region, confess to the murders, revealing that he'd concealed the bodies in the concrete of nearby Highway 210.

Since then, this dried-out dam, its diabolical rock and disturbing tunnel have continued to fascinate fans of the paranormal. Ron Hubbard died in 1986, but the Church of Scientology headquarters with its recognizable blue façade is still based in Los Angeles.

ANCIENT FOREST IN DESCANSO GARDENS ⑰

Plants from the age of dinosaurs

Descanso Gardens
1418 Descanso Drive, La Cañada Flintridge
+1 (818) 949-4200
descansogardens.org
Daily 9am–5pm

This stroll along the paths through the heart of some of the most beautiful gardens around is like a trip back in time. Way, way back ...

The botanical gardens in this park were created in 1957 by a group of enthusiasts. As you head left on the path leading to the heights, the ferns become denser, the vegetation more humid and the atmosphere heavier, a feeling both peaceful and haunting. A collection of cycads, those plants with mysterious shapes somewhere between palms and conifers, then stand before you as they stood 200 million years ago in the Jurassic period, on this patch of land first trodden by dinosaurs, then mammoths and saber-toothed tigers. Tree ferns, ginkgo, and redwoods complete this Ancient Forest, opened in 2015 thanks to donations from Katia and Frederick Elsea of La Cañada Flintridge, a community at the foot of the Los Angeles National Forest Mountains, the site of the gardens.

Although the garden managers are regularly called upon to take cumbersome plants off people's hands, such rarities, some of which no longer exist in the wild, are not often found within the same shelter. According to certain paleobotanists, the cycads, plants with a long fossil history, first appeared during the Paleozoic Era, or more exactly the Carboniferous Period, 354 to 323 million years ago. Thanks to a technique of preserving dormant embryos in case of major climate change, these non-flowering seed plants can lie dormant for millennia, waking up when conditions have become more tolerable. In the midst of this laboratory of ancient plant species you feel small and humble, admiring the strength of character of these warriors from several continents (Africa, Asia, the Americas, and Oceania), before walking on toward the more traditional collections of the Descanso Gardens, which include the Rose Garden, Japanese Garden, Camellia Collection, Oak Forest, California Natives (endemic plants), and Nature's Table (edible plants).

MOUNT WILSON OBSERVATORY

⑱

The mountain home of iconic telescopes

Mount Wilson Road, Angeles National Forest
mtwilson.edu
+1 (626) 440-9016
Monday–Friday 10am–5pm, Saturday and Sunday 8:30am–5pm
Closed Thanksgiving and Christmas; guided tours Saturday and Sunday at 1pm
Telescope observations by reservation only
Cosmic Café open April to November, weekends only (10am–5pm)

Though the Griffith Observatory is one of LA's must-sees, its tourist frenzy can be overwhelming at times. The much more intimate Mount Wilson Observatory, north of Pasadena (5,715 feet above sea level), offers an ideal substitute for lovers of starry skies. The atmospheric conditions, well away from the megalopolis, are much more conducive to astronomy. Its reputation as a pillar of modern observational cosmology is legendary.

It was here, in fact, that American astronomer Edwin Hubble discovered the phenomenon of the expansion of the universe, known as the "Hubble-Lemaître law," in 1929 (a finding that led a few decades later to the Big Bang theory). Mount Wilson, founded by George Ellery Hale in 1904, also houses the 100-inch Hooker Telescope, which for many years was the largest aperture telescope in the world.

"Here, during WWI, Harlow Shapley measured the size of the Milky Way Galaxy for the first time and located our position in it, far from the center," says the online guide, which is packed with fascinating details, just like the site itself, where conferences, thematic guided tours and even classical music concerts are regularly held inside the dome. Nearby, a number of hiking trails offer breathtaking views of the San Gabriel Mountains.

French cheese in orbit

SpaceX
Rocket Road, Hawthorne
spacex.com
+1 (310) 363-6000
Site visits only for those accompanied by a SpaceX employee

In 2010, a wheel of *brouère*, a cows'-milk cheese from the Vosges in eastern France, achieved legendary status after secretly circling the Earth twice aboard a test flight of the American aerospace company SpaceX's *Dragon* capsule.

"If you like Monty Python, you'll like our secret," explained CEO Elon Musk, revealing that his inspiration was a sketch where John Cleese walks into a shop and tries to buy only cheeses with unlikely names – before concluding that the shop doesn't sell cheese after all.

Since then, the wheel of cheese (whose label features the rubber boots-sporting cow on the poster for the 1984 movie *Top Secret!*) has been on display at SpaceX's premises.

But only the employees get to see it every day. So you'll have to get one of them to accompany you inside.

BRIDGE TO NOWHERE HIKE

⑲

A bridge that goes nowhere

Camp Bonita Road
San Gabriel Mountains National Monument, Azusa
Always accessible

Hiking is a way of life in Los Angeles, so no wonder the locals and tourists don't just roam around the city parks on the weekend. Although many outdoor-lovers stick to the paths of Griffith Park or run alongside stars in leggings at Runyon Canyon, others prefer to think outside the box.

The Bridge to Nowhere hike, north-east of the city, often overlooked because it's hard to get to but popular with a few seasoned Angelenos, offers a different option. The round trip of about 10 miles, with 900 feet of elevation change, crosses various landscapes from forest to canyon before reaching the culmination – the legendary Bridge to Nowhere.

To tackle this six-hour hike, you'll need walking boots, sunscreen, and a free permit that can be picked up at East Fork Ranger Station or Heaton Flats Trail Camp. All along the route, hikers have to ford the river, testing their balance on logs or jumping from one rock to another. There's a path alongside the water where you can stop for a picnic or swim, depending on the water level. Or take an alternate, more bucolic yet steep slope up to the heights, where succulent plants, yuccas, and wildflowers grow. All the trails – and there are many – lead to the Bridge to Nowhere.

The name is explicit enough, as the arched bridge literally doesn't lead to anything. Built in 1936, it was part of a project to link the town of Azusa, Los Angeles Country, through the San Gabriel Mountains to the mountain resort of Wrightwood to the north, elevation 5,935 feet. But in the spring of 1938, a massive flood washed out the connecting roads, sparing the bridge. Due to a lack of financial investment, the roads were never rebuilt.

At the trailhead you'll find the remains of this East Fork Road. The bridge, free of traffic, has also become a popular destination for bungee jumpers (only on weekends), this being the only spot of its kind in all of California.

MOUNT BALDY ZEN CENTER

⑳

Zen Center where Leonard Cohen became a Buddhist monk

7901 Mount Baldy Road
mbzc.org
+1 (909) 985 6410

In the far east of Los Angeles County, right on the border with San Bernardino County, Mount Baldy emerges from the trees of Angeles National Forest. Before reaching the resort, a ski station perched on this treeless mountain, you'll come across a series of incredible trails, including the famous Bridge to Nowhere (see page 202).

But this mysterious mountain also serves as a backdrop for MBZC, the Mount Baldy Zen Center, a monastery that teaches Rinzai, one of the three schools of Zen Buddhism.

This group of little wooden cabins from a former Scout camp, purchased in 1971 by Kyozan Joshi Sasaki, a Japanese Zen master and *roshi* ("venerated teacher") born in 1907, has become the main temple in the region.

After keeping a low profile for many years, the monastery was swept into the spotlight when, after several short stays, Canadian musician

and poet Leonard Cohen joined it in 1993 for a six-year retreat, during which he was ordained as a monk. "When we stop constantly thinking about ourselves, a certain feeling of tranquility overwhelms us," he declared at the time, admitting to having spent 30 years of his life studying Zen Buddhism before taking the plunge.

Under the name Jikan, he cooked, cleaned, and meditated in silence. Getting up at three in the morning to clean the washrooms or shovel the snow piling up at the doors was also part of the routine.

Cohen, who was prone to debilitating depression, ultimately left the monastery in 1999, but continued to infuse his albums with a troubled, death-obsessed Jewish spirituality. A few weeks before his death in November 2016, he explained to *The New Yorker* that he hadn't been in search of a new religion but rather that, for him, Zen was "a discipline rather than a religion, a practice of investigation."

Describing the harsh winters at the center, he said: "People have the idea that a monastery is a place of serenity and contemplation; it isn't that at all. It's a hospital, where people come to learn how to walk and speak and breathe ... it makes whining the least appropriate response to suffering." It is a life lesson that would accompany him until the end.

Things are rather different now, but the center is still no vacation spot as it continues to maintain strict respect for the precepts of the Zen Buddhist philosophy of Rinzai (including getting up at 3am).

Out of season, i.e. in spring and autumn, the center can be rented for retreats, conferences, and seminars.

© LinSu Hill de Whittier

REMAINS OF THE "SOCIALIST COLONY" OF THE LLANO DEL RIO COLLECTIVE

(21)

A communal utopia in an inhospitable desert

Llano, California
+1 (916) 445-7000
ldrg.wordpress.com
Site always accessible

North of Angeles National Forest, about 18 miles southeast of Palmdale, the road that leads from Santa Clarita to Las Vegas gives an unexpected glimpse of a row of stone chimneys. Surrounded by a few walls broken down by the ravages of time are the outlines of a village.

What first comes to mind is an old abandoned hotel, or a kind of ghost town from which the last residents had suddenly fled, scared off

one fine morning by this over-arid climate. In fact, for a few years this desolate spot was home to one of the most astonishing (and short-lived) utopias of the 20th century.

Imagine, over a hundred years ago, up to 1,500 people living frugally, first in 200 tents and then in adobe shelters built from stones they unearthed, around a community center where the impressive hearths are all that remain. Under the leadership of Job Harriman, a repeatedly unsuccessful socialist candidate for governor of California and mayor of Los Angeles, hundreds of families moved to this corner of the desert from 1914 onwards with the idea of founding a society that would follow the principles of sharing and mutual aid. Though it was arid, there was a water source nearby,

Each prospective resident was to acquire a piece of land in exchange for community-oriented work. "We will build a town and houses for many homeless families", Harriman promised. "We will show the world that it is possible to live without war, without greed, without rent, and without profit."

For a year, his socialist (or Communist, depending on your point of view) dream survived as best it could, supported by an accommodating banker friend and curious tourists. But the general assemblies meant to manage this idealistic collective soon turned into an opportunity to settle scores with the omniscient "patriarch." Neighboring farmers began to complain about intensive use of the only water source, and the local press looked down on the project. The hard life and spartan comforts did the rest: by 1915, half the families had left this "ranch" of ill fortune, disappointed. Some even sued Harriman.

The indomitable remainder did however manage to establish a relatively balanced mini-society as an autonomous village, until 1917. From grocery store to laundromat, soap maker to library, infirmary to carpenter's shop, by way of the school, of course (inspired by the Montessori Method), all trades were represented. *Brave New World* author Aldous Huxley even visited the community as a neighbor and penned a laudatory article.

But this second honeymoon was also temporary. Access to water being the key to success in this part of the world, the Californian authorities' refusal to allow a dam to be built (and thus ensure good harvests), was the fatal blow to Job Harriman's utopia. He finally moved to Louisiana, abandoning the last residents to their sad fate – which didn't last long either: by the beginning of 1918 everyone had left.

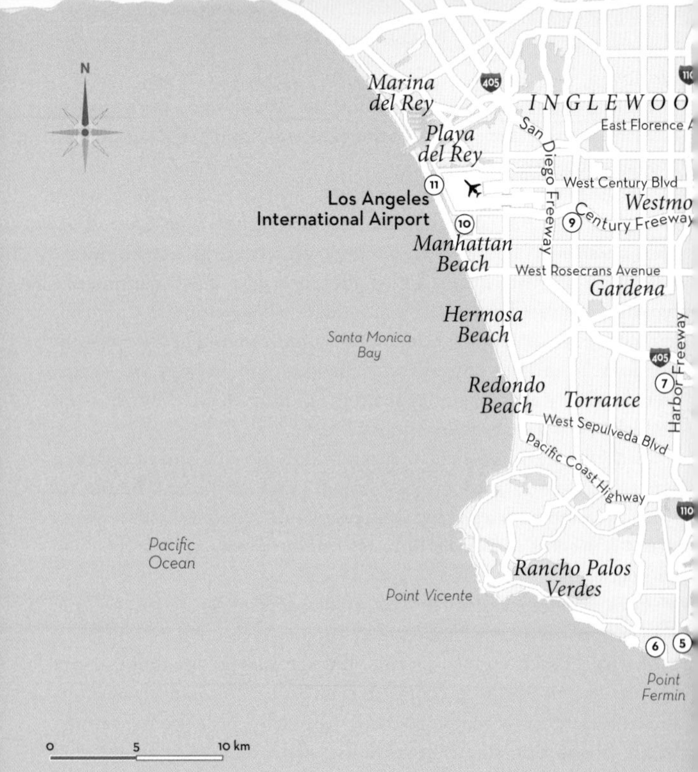

South L.A.

① VINELAND DRIVE-IN THEATER *210*

② HAZEL WRIGHT MEMORIAL ORGAN IN THE "CRYSTAL CATHEDRAL" *212*

③ RIVO ALTO CIRCULAR CANAL *216*

④ BISON ON THE LOOSE ON CATALINA ISLAND *218*

⑤ ANGELS GATE PARK AND FORT MACARTHUR MILITARY MUSEUM *220*

⑥ SUNKEN CITY OF SAN PEDRO *222*

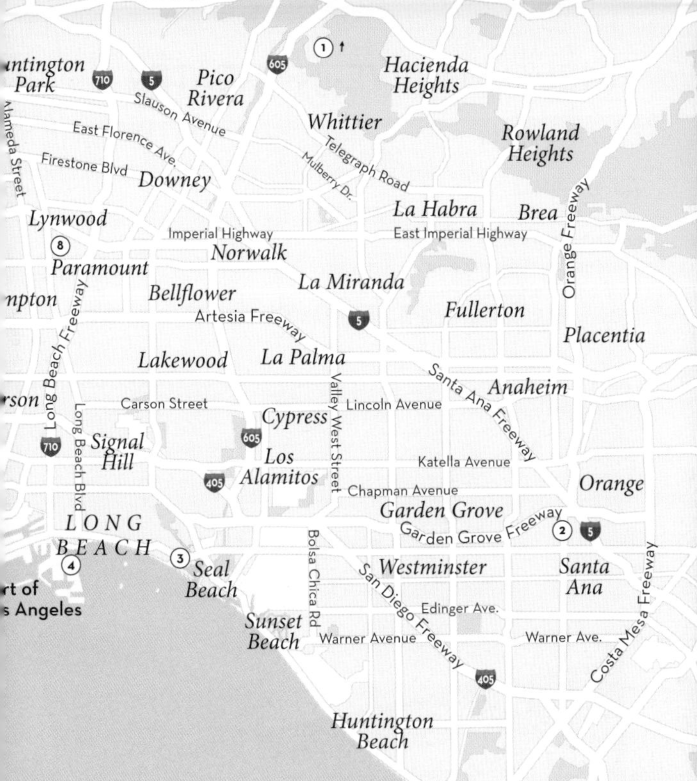

⑦ BAVARIAN VILLAGE OF TORRANCE 224
⑧ ANGELES ABBEY MEMORIAL PARK CEMETERY 226
⑨ BEACH BOYS CHILDHOOD HOME 228
⑩ OLD TOWN MUSIC HALL 230
⑪ THE ABANDONED TOWN OF SURFRIDGE 232

VINELAND DRIVE-IN THEATER

1

L.A. nostalgia

443 N. Vineland Ave.
City of Industry
(+1) 626-961-9262
vinelanddriveintheater.com
feedback@vinelanddriveintheater.com
7 days a week. Gates open at 7pm, show starts at dusk

An industrial and retail park serving as an urban hub, the City of Industry is rather lacking in charm but is nevertheless home to the Vineland Theater, one of the few remaining drive-in theaters in Southern California.

Open for business since April 15, 1955, it has survived throughout the decades and the changing fashions of the Seventh Art. Operations Manager Juan Gonzales has held out against the times with his staff, maintaining the large complex's four lots. Many changes have been made over the years, but the experience is much the same as it was six decades ago when the first cars rolled onto the lot. There have been improvements, of course, most notably the disappearance of the speakers that once screamed into the cars; now, sound is received via car radio (107.7 on the FM dial, to be specific), harnessing the power of any car's stereo system for this cinematic experience that is at once communal and personal.

There is a certain sort of nostalgia in Los Angeles that sometimes manifests itself in a love for big, chrome-trimmed vintage cars, drive-in mini-burgers and strawberry milkshakes. In a time when the city's car-reliant culture is being called into doubt, the question remains as to whether this cultural vision is regressive in Los Angeles' current evolution. Yet, the car has formed the core of many of the city's communal traditions. The drive-in has traditionally provided a rare place of interaction, where movie viewing is practically secondary to the overall social experience.

When the movie industry announced the abandonment of 35mm projection in favor of digital, it tolled a death knell for many of the nation's drive-in theaters. With a cost of $80,000 per digital screen, it seemed like the Vineland Theater's fate was sealed. Fortunately, the money came in. The upgrade took place in June 2013 and, for one of the few times in its history, the Vineland was sold out on all four screens. The tradition of surrendering to the Hollywood magic while under the stars and in your car survives, at the cost of just $10 a head. For a mere pittance, you too can bring your whole family, round up your buddies, or bundle up under a blanket with your sweetheart and enjoy the old-fashioned charm of a Saturday night double feature.

HAZEL WRIGHT MEMORIAL ORGAN IN THE "CRYSTAL CATHEDRAL"

②

A unique instrument in an incredible setting

Christ Cathedral – 13280 Chapman Avenue, Garden Grove
christcathedralcalifornia.org – +1 (714) 971-2141
Saturday from 3:30pm, Sunday all day

Technically, this amazing cathedral and its sublime organ aren't in LA, nor even in Los Angeles County, but farther south in Garden Grove, Orange County.

The Crystal Cathedral, originally a megachurch belonging to the Rev. Robert Schuller, a popular 1980s televangelist, was acquired in 2011 by the Roman Catholic Diocese of Orange. The building was renovated and reopened in July 2019 as Christ Cathedral. A 1,000-pound metal cross, Carrara marble altar, and reflective panels make the building as bright inside as outside. Mass is celebrated in English, Spanish, Vietnamese, and Chinese every Saturday and Sunday.

The renovators even had the good taste not to install an overly modern organ. Once inside the cathedral, exceptional in itself, the Hazel Wright Memorial Organ, one of the most imposing in the world, steals the show. Designed and installed here in 1977 by the Fratelli Ruffatti company, it consists of 270 ranks (sets of pipes) comprising over 16,000 individual pipes, all controlled by one of the largest consoles ever built.

During the cathedral makeover, the organ was even sent to Italy for repairs, before returning four years later to ring out again in its final home; its reassembly took more than a year. "The pipes were infested with termites and insects," diocese organist John Romeri told the press. "The magnificent trumpet pipes were eaten away. Some pipes had distorted or collapsed because of the heat." Now in an air-conditioned, quake-proof space where the humidity is also controlled, the instrument is well-protected.

Arvella Schuller, wife of the TV pastor, was the driving force behind the installation of a spectacular instrument that would be noticed during their weekly TV show, *Hour of Power*, broadcast live from Crystal Cathedral. "Hazel" was created from two other instruments: organist Virgil Fox, working with Fratelli Ruffatti, had an organ from the Lincoln Center in New York City grafted onto the equally impressive 1977 organ, which was in the local church in Garden Grove.

This hybrid was made possible at the time by a $2 million donation from benefactor Hazel Wright of Chicago, a longtime fan of Schuller's show, so the organ was named for her. At a total cost of $58 million, renovation of the Roman Catholic church has ensured the sustainability of both an incredible building and a unique instrument.

RIVO ALTO CIRCULAR CANAL

③

Italian-inspired California cool

Naples Island
Long Beach
californiabeaches.com/naples-california

The Venice canals, just behind the legendary beach of the same name, now figure among the top California tourist destinations – sometimes found by chance on quitting the choppy waves at the seafront in favor of super-cool Abbot Kinney Boulevard (named after the real estate developer of this stretch of coast). But, some 35 miles further south along the shore towards the Port of Long Beach, there's a better-preserved gem that would probably win the prize for the most perfect picture postcard of Southern California life.

Located on the island-enclave of Naples, east of the already charming Belmont Shore, the Rivo Alto circular canal has its own park and the most exclusive properties around, surrounded by a mini-beach that's unbelievably peaceful, as if photogenic and unpretentious weren't enough.

The houses, of various architectural styles and Italian-sounding names, are strung out alongside a boardwalk where everything is the epitome of "luxury, calm and pleasure" (along with the hefty bank balance required to live on the island). To the east is a breathtaking view of the peninsula and marina from Naples Plaza Park. Beyond, the estuary separating Long Beach from Seal Beach also marks the line between Los Angeles County and Orange County.

This developer's dream, built in 1903 on marshland near the artificial Alamitos Bay at the mouth of San Gabriel River, was completed in 1920. It was destroyed in the 1933 earthquake but later rebuilt. Of course, to fulfill the fantasy of reproducing (still today) a miniature Californian Venice in glossy perfection, a single company offers gondola rides and floating dining just like in Italy, striped shirts and gondoliers included. Yet they are rare enough not to disturb your stroll through this neighborhood where few tourists stray.

In addition, unlike the Venetian canals, here you can hire a kayak or paddle boat, or even swim. A sea of tranquility.

BISON ON THE LOOSE ON CATALINA ISLAND

④

A herd of extras

+1 (310) 510-1445
catalinaconservancy.org
Accessible year-round
A ferry, the Catalina Express, runs once every 2 hours from Long Beach, twice daily from Dana Point (five times a day in the summer), and three times a day from San Pedro (once an hour in the summer)
$74.50 round trip for adults, $59 for children under 11
Tip: plan an overnight stay at one of the Avalon hotels

Only the crazy local film industry could conjure up the sight of 150 bison quietly grazing in the middle of (Santa) Catalina Island.

The bison, a hybrid of wild and domestic cattle, were brought in by Hollywood in 1924 as ... extras. In fact the only species endemic to this island 22 miles west of San Pedro are mice, squirrels, foxes, birds, and a few invertebrates.

So these beasts were "imported" for the filming of George B. Seitz's pro-American Indian western *The Vanishing American* (a remake with the same title starring Scott Brady was released in the 1950s). In an ironic twist, the footage of them was edited out – you don't see hide nor hair of them in the movie.

Although some 100 years later the bison now roam free on the island, they're still considered domesticated and have turned into one of Catalina's main tourist attractions.

The island's protection agency, the Catalina Island Conservancy, has been overseeing the herds since 1972, controlling their numbers and communicating on their well-being and the importance of their presence.

Responsible eco-tours are offered to tourists who venture out to the island's shores (private cars are prohibited). The secret is well guarded, as these closely supervised wild lands welcome a relatively small number of visitors each year.

The herd numbers 150, precisely the number of bison the island comfortably can shelter without harming other fauna and flora. Births have been regulated since the contraceptive program resumed in 2009. With luck, you might see a newborn calf gamboling with its mother on what will be an unforgettable outing, far, far away from the din of the megalopolis.

ANGELS GATE PARK AND FORT MACARTHUR MILITARY MUSEUM

⑤

A hazardous offensive during WWII

Angels Gate Park
3601 S. Gaffey Street, San Pedro
From sunrise to sunset

If one walks to the edge of the bluffs of Angels Gate Park and peers downward, a curious sight awaits the urban explorer. Concrete steps lead to a semi-circular structure with high walls resembling an ancient theater. They are the remains of Battery Osgood-Farley. Built between 1916 and 1919 to defend Los Angeles harbor and Fort MacArthur, they once housed 14-inch disappearing guns capable of firing 1,560-pound projectiles over 14 miles into the Catalina Channel. They soon became more of a nuisance to the local population, however, since their firing often rattled and blew out windows in many nearby residences. By World War II, changes in warfare made them essentially obsolete. Despite the ineffectiveness of the big guns, Angels Gate was still a location of strategic importance, receiving additional artillery during the global conflict. Smaller anti-aircraft guns were installed to reinforce important sites up and down the coast. Far from the main theater of action, the guns remained silent for most of the war, with one notable exception. On the night of February 24 and 25, 1942, the guns were fired with all their might. What they were defending themselves against has remained a source of debate and discussion ever since, however. Quickly dubbed "The Battle of Los Angeles," the action that night saw the firing of over 1,400 12.5-pound anti-aircraft shells at a series of unidentified objects in the air.

Following an earlier submarine attack on a Santa Barbara refinery, the West Coast was on alert. Reports of glowing or blinking lights in the air along the coast caused a blackout to be ordered. Objects were detected on radar, placing the anti-aircraft batteries on alert, and at around 3 a.m. the city's artillery opened fire, causing a deafening roar throughout the vast expanses of the Los Angeles basin. Despite reports of aircraft by some witnesses, no bombs were dropped on the city and not a single craft was shot down. What was seen in the skies remains a mystery, although evidence gathered by more reliable witnesses in the "battle's" aftermath pointed to a more probable cause. Air balloons, supposedly utilized by radar crews in Santa Monica to test their newly installed equipment, had wandered off course. The pervading fear did the rest.

The over-reaction that took place that night in 1942 has since been criticized, derided, and lampooned, most famously in Stephen Spielberg's zany comedy, *1941*. However, though we may laugh at it now, World War II did cause great fear and paranoia among the citizens of Los Angeles, traces of which can still be seen in old blacked-out windows and the few concrete defenses that dot the coast. Yet few places illustrate the full extent of Los Angeles' preparedness for war more than Angels Gate Park and the adjoining Fort MacArthur Museum.

SUNKEN CITY OF SAN PEDRO

⑥

A neighborhood swallowed by the ocean

500 West Paseo Del Mar, San Pedro

The vast Santa Monica Bay encompasses most of the Pacific Rim of Los Angeles County, which runs from Malibu to Long Beach. At the southern tip, Palos Verdes and San Pedro occupy Point Vicente and Point Firmin (with its pretty Lightouse), perhaps the most charming and authentic corners of California in this sprawling city whose pace exhausts visitors and locals alike, especially when they're stuck in traffic. Here in San Pedro, despite the proximity of one of the biggest seaports in the country, life is lived at a slower pace.

After you've seen the lighthouse and the Korean Friendship Bell, head for the site of a landslide that carried off homes and roadways in 1929. It has become a pilgrimage for romantic teenagers, lovers of beautiful sunset photographs, graffiti artists titillated by the challenge, and, increasingly, urban explorers (urbexers).

Unofficially known as the "Sunken City," this neighborhood, covering 40,000 square feet, was swallowed up by the tumultuous ocean. Its remaining 1920s bungalows and other cliffside homes, along with part of the park, would have gradually disappeared at the rate of a foot a day if they hadn't been relocated.

Ever since the local authorities erected a fence to prevent accidents, all that can be seen from the road are a few flattened walls (those of two homes that couldn't be saved in time), roofs, chunks of sidewalk, remains of railings and obstinate palm trees. Of course, curious visitors sometimes climb over the fence, risking a $1,000 fine for the thrill of standing on the cliff's edge and getting a closer look.

Over the years proposals and petitions have asked for the site to be reopened to the public, at least during the day, even if that means policing by night. "Sunken City," technically still a public park, has become a tourist mecca repeatedly featured in ads, movies, TV shows, and skateboarding videos. But, after complaints from local residents about late-night partying and violent incidents, the mayor has limited access until a lasting solution can be found. Given the low deterrent power of the fencing, a compromise is under consideration. "We are working with the Department of Recreation and Parks, engineers and other city departments," a local council member recently declared, "to create and adopt a plan to clean up sections of the Sunken City, to make it safer and a legal extension of Point Fermin Park once again."

BAVARIAN VILLAGE OF TORRANCE

⑦

A taste of Germany in Southern California

Alpine village
833 West Torrance Boulevard, Torrance
+1 (310) 327-4384
alpinevillagecenter.com
Monday–Thursday 10am–7pm, Friday, Saturday and Sunday 9am–7pm (village, market and cafe)

Little Persia, Koreatown, Little Tokyo, Historic Filipinotown, Little Armenia – in a county as diverse as Los Angeles, where each country's diaspora has forged its culture in well-defined neighborhoods, it's no surprise to find markets offering specialties from communities worldwide. But with the exception of Chinatown and Little Tokyo, homesickness doesn't extend to reproducing the architectural and landscape elements of one's home country.

Although some German personalities invested in Brentwood and Pacific Palisades after Hitler took power in 1933 (Thomas Mann, Bertolt Brecht, Fritz Lang), strictly speaking there's no German district in LA. But wait ...

Since 1968, a quaint site has been giving German buffs their taste of nostalgia – and not only during Oktoberfest, the now world-famous beer festival celebrated in Munich and elsewhere on the first Saturday after Sept. 15. From the inimitable sausages to "local" pastries, jewelry, and souvenirs, the Alpine Village market is stocked with otherwise unobtainable European goods.

But it isn't the shopping that interests us here: this concentration of southern German culture includes appealing examples of Alpine architecture, in abrupt contrast to the unattractive strip mall-like surroundings alongside Highway 110.

Alpine Village, open every day of the year, is actually a reproduction of an authentic Bavarian village with a chapel, balconies and typical courtyards, at the heart of which little shops offer curious visitors a range of imported products. Though recently threatened with demolition by a developer after a few years of decline (the main restaurant closed in April 2020, Oktoberfest 2019 was more restricted, and the shrinking clientele is advancing in age), the village should soon be listed as a historic monument by Los Angeles County.

ANGELES ABBEY MEMORIAL PARK CEMETERY

(8)

A replica of the Taj Mahal dome, a mosque ...

1515 East Compton Boulevard, Compton
+1 (310) 631-1141
Daily 8am–4:30pm

The Incorruptibles, *Alias*, *Constantine*, *JAG* – in the 1990s and 2000s, many Hollywood superhero films and TV dramas used Compton cemetery as a backdrop. However, the scenes featuring the cemetery don't reveal the life of this deprived district in south LA, but ersatz streets of Casablanca, Cairo, Calcutta, or some undefined place allegedly in the Middle East, or even more vaguely in Asia.

And for good reason: with its Taj Mahal dome replica, commissioned in 1923 by ship-owner George Craig (who sent two of his employees to India looking for inspiration), the cemetery of Angeles Abbey Memorial Park is nothing like a traditional American necropolis. Its four mausoleums mix Byzantine, Moorish, and Spanish influences with the Mughal style of crypts and dome, characteristic of the famous palace at Agra that combines Ottoman, Iranian, and Indian architectural elements. Inside, the Islamic influence is even clearer, with its tiled vaults.

Paradoxically, inside one of the white marble mausoleums is a chapel with a decrepit old organ. The chapel's stained-glass windows are a reproduction of *L'Angelus*, a moving painting by Jean-François Millet displayed at the Musée d'Orsay in Paris. Faced with such a heterogeneous collection, you could be in any country in the world.

As David Reid recalls in his very personal book *Sex, Death and God in L.A.*, "It wasn't too long ago that finding a plot to bury a black body posed a problem in Los Angeles. In some areas, private charters blocked these interments [in the cemeteries reserved for whites, ed.] as late as 1966. African-American families, in black veils and ash-gray suits, loaded caskets onto streetcars and rode to Evergreen Cemetery in East L.A."

Shortly after the Compton cemetery was inaugurated in 1923, you could say that this piece of land was a rural retreat where white families had migrated, away from bustling LA and the Port of Long Beach.

But the city of Compton went through a turbulent period when impoverishment, gang culture and corruption gradually changed the city, turning what had become a black, middle-class enclave in the 1960s and 1970s into a ghetto with a sulfurous reputation and rampant crime rate, one of the highest in the U.S. The climax of this tragic tale was the riots of 1992, which, though they didn't start here, spread with alarming ease.

Three generations of the Sanders family, now headed by Jean, have managed one of the largest historically black cemeteries in the country, in a city now predominantly Latino. And Compton, more at peace than in the past, slowly continues to change. The "fake Taj Mahal" is still there.

BEACH BOYS CHILDHOOD HOME

⑨

Feel the Good Vibrations

Beach Boys Historic Landmark
3701 West 119th Street, Hawthorne

Southeast of LAX airport, wedged between highways 405 and 105, the town of Hawthorne – named after New England author Nathaniel Hawthorne – perfectly fulfills its role as residential soft underbelly of Los Angeles County. Even its motto is "City of Good Neighbors."

Here, very close to the present-day Century Freeway, as Interstate 105 is known, a family of musicians grew up: the Beach Boys. In addition to revolutionizing the history of music, they basically linked their rise to fame to the State of California through the surf rock that was so popular in the early 1960s.

Brian, Carl, and Dennis Wilson lived together with their parents on a since-demolished housing estate where they are now commemorated by a monument, relatively far from the beaches that made them famous. Accompanied by their cousin Mike Love and friend Al Jardine, the blond troubadours composed their first singles in Hawthorne, including their breakthrough song *Surfin'*, at a time when their albums were filled with hymns to the sweetness of life and of girls sprawled on the sand. It would be a few years before Brian Wilson chiseled out a much more complex and dazzling popular music style.

The monument (a red brick and white tile reproduction of the 1963 Surfer Girl album cover) wasn't erected until 2004 – decades after the bulldozers had carved out the freeway. The California State Historic Resources Commission, backed by the Rock & Roll Hall of Fame, had to put it to the vote, to turn the place where the house once stood into a historic site dedicated to the genius of a unique band.

On the day the memorial was unveiled, Brian Wilson and Al Jardine even made the trip to perform two tracks in front of 800 rapturous fans.

This modest site is in the heart of a residential zone where hundreds of families live, with not much parking available: we advise passing through discreetly and quickly.

OLD TOWN MUSIC HALL

⑩

A centenarian organ accompanying old silent movies

140 Richmond Street
El Segundo
+1 (310) 322-2592
oldtownmusichall.org
Open during performances, generally Friday and Saturday around 8pm, and Saturday and Sunday around 2:30pm (full program available on website)
Tickets on sale at site only

An authentic journey back in time starts as soon as you push open the doors of the Old Town Music Hall in the heart of downtown El Segundo, a municipality close to LAX airport. It's a charming neighborhood with a calm ambiance. Behind the green frontage, recalling an updated saloon bar, is an old-fashioned foyer giving onto a small theater with red draperies and huge chandeliers, like in a Western movie.

Since 1968, this unique theater has not only projected old silent and sound movie classics, it also hosts jazz and ragtime concerts, thanks to a gigantic 2,600-pipe organ dubbed the Mighty Wurlitzer, dating from 1925. It's the most imposing instrument ever built by the Rudolph Wurlitzer Company of Cincinnati.

The theater offers Laurel and Hardy cycles and, around Halloween, a festival of horror classics, conferences with specialists in vintage animation and Fred Astaire or the Three Stooges retrospectives, all usually with live musical accompaniment as when they were first shown.

When the films are not silent, however, a few tunes are played before each showing. In December, a mass karaoke featuring American culture's most iconic Christmas carols is organized around the Wurlitzer. It's hard to be more nostalgically original.

The team of enthusiasts who run the Old Town Music Hall as a non-profit association also sometimes concoct delicious coconut macaroons, sold in boxes, instead of ubiquitous popcorn. It's all about savoring this timeless interlude until the final curtain.

THE ABANDONED TOWN OF SURFRIDGE

(11)

Traces of a lost town

Between Vista del Mar and Pershing Drive – LAX Airport

Travelers to and from Los Angeles International Airport (LAX) may not notice traces of a suburban development long ago abandoned, wrapping around the runways on the western and northern edges of the airport. This was the community of Surfridge, which has sat uninhabited for the last five decades. Crumbling concrete foundations and the occasional sign and streetlamp are now the only evidence that the area was once a thriving neighborhood. It is said that until recently the streetlamps would still light up.

The abandonment of Surfridge is connected with the boom of commercial aviation after WWII, which necessitated an expansion of LAX into surrounding communities. Three new runways put the flightpath directly on top of Surfridge. With further proposals for expansion on the horizon, the city of Los Angeles decided to enact its right of eminent domain and acquire the property. From 1965 to 1979, 800 homes were demolished in conjunction with the relocation of 2,000 residents.

The legacy of Surfridge remains mixed. With expansive views, it was once a haven for the city's wealthy, amongst them the mighty director

Cecil B. DeMille. For some, it was a paradise, embodying all of the ideals of the romantic Southern California dream: Mission style stucco houses, palm tress waving in the salty air, and the beach just a few steps away from the front door. For others, however, it represented the removal of blemish from the city's segregated past. Surfridge was originally established as a Caucasian-only community in the 1920s. The development's deed contained restrictions excluding those "not entirely of the Caucasion race except such as are in the employ of the resident owners." Houses, too, were required to obey rigid standards: exteriors in stucco were the rule while wood was forbidden. Conformity to an imposed "ideal" of Southern California's coastal lifestyle was therefore enforced by regulation.

Various redevelopment proposals were passed by city and airport officials in the 1980s, but all were voted down by the California Coastal Commission. As fate would have it, the former town of Surfridge was a natural habitat for the endangered El Segundo Blue Butterfly. Since this revelation, the city-run butterfly preserve at Surfridge has enabled a significant comeback for the species, whose population has increased from a mere 500 to 125,000. The Coastal Commission is responsible for the ongoing return of 48 acres of Surfridge to its natural state.

Despite the intermittent cry of jet engines overhead, humanity still attempts to inhabit this place. The recent demolition of some of the sidewalks and streets, and the gradual takeover of the bluff by sage, poppies, and salt grass, confirms that Surfridge is still an example of what was once a rarity in Los Angeles: the retreat of development.

10 steepest streets in the USA *139*
Abandoned sets from *M*A*S*H* *134*
Abandoned town of Surfridge *232*
Adventurer's Club of Los Angeles meeting room *60*
Alfred Hitchcock's bungalow 5195 *154*
Ancient forest in the Descanso Gardens *198*
Angeles Abbey Memorial Park Cemetery *226*
Angels Gate Park and Fort Macarthur military museum *220*
Another firefighter museum *15*
Aoyama fig tree *24*
Armenian Genocide Memorial tears *186*
Bare-chested Abraham Lincoln statue *28*
Bavarian village of Torrance *224*
Baxter Street *138*
Beach Boys childhood home *228*
Belmont abandoned tunnel dog park *46*
Berlin Wall Segments *90*
Biddy Mason Memorial Park *36*
Big Lebowski aparment *118*
Bison on the loose on Catalina Island *218*
Blue Ribbon Garden *44*
Bridge to nowhere hike *202*
Bungalow Heaven neighborhood *184*
California's only other Statue of Liberty *19*
Camouflaged offshore oil platforms *97*
Cardiff Tower *96*
Celluloid Monument *98*
Charles Bukowski's bungalow *74*
Chicken Boy *172*
Church of the Angels bell *178*
Clay sculptures at the Bhagavad-Gita Museum *114*
Coca-Cola "Ocean Liner" *12*
Colorado Street suicide bridge *188*
Constance and Carl Bigsby's "Missile Grave" *76*
Crossroads of the World *13*
"Devil's Gate" dam *196*
Donald C. Tillman water reclamation plant *160*
Door to room A113 of Calarts *162*
Eagle Rock *190*
Eames House *130*
Echo Park's Time Traval Mart *52*
Finnish Folk Art Museum – Pasadena Museum of History *192*
Forgotten details of the Million Dollar Theatre façade *38*
French cheese in orbit *201*
"Happy Foot/Sad Foot" sign at Silverlake *70*
Hidden Steps, an institution for all LA sporty types *55*
Faces of Elysian Valley *58*
First red carpet in history *39*
Franck Gehry residence *128*
Frederick R. Weisman Art Foundation *104*
"Freedom Boulevard " building by Thierry Noir *158*
Gamble House *194*
Gas station to Starbucks *89*
Gilmore gas station at Farmers Market *88*
Graves of Carole Lombard and Clark Gable *144*
Griffith Park abandoned zoo *64*
Grunion Run *126*
Hamburger Mary's Bingo *86*
Hazel Wright memorial organ in the "Crystal Cathedral" *212*
Heritage Square Museum *166*
Hidden in the hair of Jackie and Mack Robinson *182*
Hidden stairs that became Hollywood stars *81*
High Tower Elevator Association *80*
Hike on the LA-96C anti-missile defense site *110*
Hiking at Murphy Ranch *132*
Hollyhock House *72*
House of Michal Jackson's *Thriller* *50*
Initials "BPOE" on the pediment of Angels Flight Railway *40*
Japanese Garden at the Doubletree hotel *22*
Joyous little sculptures on the telephone poles *17*
LA's shortest and longest streets *139*
Largest building in the world with seismic base isolation *33*

Learn how to make your own neon 147
Los Angeles Police Museum 176
Lummis Home (El Alisal) 168
Magic Castle 82
Mansion that inspired a novel that was later filmed there ... 107
Mayors' portrait gallery 32
Memorial plaques to "Room 8" The Cat 56
Monthly open day at Greystone Mansion 106
Moore laboratory of zoology 174
Mosaic Tile House 120
Mount Baldy Zen Center 204
Mount Wilson Observatory 200
Muhammad Ali's star 84
Museum of African American Firefighters 14
Museum of Death 78
Museum of Jurassic Technology 116
Museum of the Holy Land 140
Music Box Steps 54
Mysterious assassination, restaged once a year 107
Neon Museum 146
"Official" terminus of Route 66 124
O'Neill House 102
Old Town Music Hall 230
Original "Batcave" of Bronson Canyon 66
Original route of the first Campo de Cahuenga Mission 156
Other Storybook buildings 101
Our Lady of the Angels Cathedral Kindergarten 26
Pasadena's wild parrots 175
Phantasma Gloria 121
Pilgrimage for Dude fans 119
Plaque marquing the exact center of the city 108
Police Academy cafe: dinner with the cops, open to the public 177
Remains of the "Socialist Colony" of the Llano del Rio Collective 206
Rivo Alto circular canal 216
Runway of disused Grand Central Air Terminal 148
Sacred water source of the Tongva 112
Secrets of Pasadena's giant fork 180
Self-Realization Fellowship Lake Shrine 170
Shakespeare Bridge 68
Shumei Hollywood Center 171
Silverlake neighborhood on foot 71
South Keystone Street 150
Statue of Chiune Sugihara 20
Statue of Liberty copies and tributes 18
Street that used to be an airport runway 149
SuihoEn, The Japanese Garden 161
Sunken City of San Pedro 222
Symbolism of the city's heraldic seal 35
Synchronized swimmers at the Dolby Theatre 85
Take a Neon Cruise 147
Triforium 30
Two other "Young Lincolns" 29
UCLA's impressive collection of meteorites 61
Venice Beach rainbow lifeguard station 122
Vineland drive-in theater 210
Vista Hermosa Park 48
Walk alongside the Los Angeles River 142
Walt's barn 152
Warner mural in Wilshire Boulevard synagogue 92
Wells Fargo History Museum 42
Williams Andrews Clark Memorial library 94
"Witch's House" 100

NOTES

It was September 1995 and Thomas Jonglez was in Peshawar, the northern Pakistani city 20 kilometres from the tribal zone he was to visit a few days later. It occurred to him that he should record the hidden aspects of his native city, Paris, which he knew so well. During his seven-month trip back home from Beijing, the countries he crossed took in Tibet (entering clandestinely, hidden under blankets in an overnight bus), Iran and Kurdistan. He never took a plane but travelled by boat, train or bus, hitchhiking, cycling, on horseback or on foot, reaching Paris just in time to celebrate Christmas with the family.

On his return, he spent two fantastic years wandering the streets of the capital to gather material for his first "secret guide", written with a friend. For the next seven years he worked in the steel industry until the passion for discovery overtook him. He launched Jonglez Publishing in 2003 and moved to Venice three years later. In 2013, in search of new adventures, the family left Venice and spent six months travelling to Brazil, via North Korea, Micronesia, the Solomon Islands, Easter Island, Peru and Bolivia. After seven years in Rio de Janeiro, he now lives in Berlin with his wife and three children.

Jonglez Publishing produces a range of titles in nine languages, released in 40 countries.

ACKNOWLEDGEMENTS

The authors would like to thank all of the Los Angelenos (friends, acquaintances and those they met for a brief, special moment) who, thanks to their excellent advice, helped create this guidebook.
Our warmest thanks to Sandra Cazenave for her support.

CREDITS

Unless noted otherwise, all texts and photos are by Félicien Cassan and Darrow Carson, except for:

Texts:
Zac Pennington: The *Triforium*, Music Box Steps, Museum of Jurrassic Technology
Sandra Cazenave: Walk alongside the Los Angeles River, Walt's Barn, Bridge to Nowhere hike
Albert Lopez: Vineland Drive-In Theater, Angels Gate Park and Fort Macarthur military museum
Michelle Young: The abandoned town of Surfridge

Photos:
Zac Pennington : The *Triforium*, Music Box Steps, Museum of Jurrassic Technology (left photo)
Mike Hume: Forgotten details of the Million Dollar Theatre façade, Hidden in the hair of Jackie and Mack Robinson, Angels Gate Park and Fort Macarthur military museum.
James Bartlett: Celluloid Monument
Sandra Cazenave: Walk alongside the Los Angeles River, Walt's Barn, Bridge to Nowhere hike
Catalina Island Conservancy: Bison on the loose on Catalina Island
Michelle Young: The abandoned town of Surfridge

Maps: Cyrille Suss – **Layout:** Emmanuelle Willard Toulemonde – **Translation:** Caroline Lawrence – **Copy-editing:** Sue Pollack – **Proofreading:** Kimberly Bess – **Publishing:** Clémence Mathé